WHEN SKATEBOARDS WILL BE FREE

WHEN SKATEBOARDS WILL BE FREE

a memoir of a political childhood

saïd sayrafiezadeh

the dial press

WHEN SKATEBOARDS WILL BE FREE
A Dial Press Book / April 2009

Published by The Dial Press
A Division of Random House, Inc.
New York, New York

Portions of this book appeared in different form in *Granta*.

Book design by Ginger Legato

The Dial Press is a registered trademark of Random House, Inc., and the colophon
is a trademark of Random House, Inc.

Library of Congress Cataloging-in-Publication Data
Sayrafiezadeh, Saïd.
When skateboards will be free : a memoir of a political childhood / Saïd Sayrafiezadeh.
p.   cm.
ISBN 978-0-385-34068-7 (hardcover)—ISBN 978-0-440-33839-0 (e-book).
1. Sayrafiezadeh, Saïd—Childhood and youth.   2. Socialists—United States—Biography.
3. Socialist Workers Party.   I. Title.
HX84.S39A3 2009
324.273'7—dc22
[B]
2008051096

Printed in the United States of America
Published simultaneously in Canada

www.dialpress.com

10 9 8 7 6 5 4 3 2 1
BVG

To Karen Mainenti and Steven Kuchuck
for their optimism

WHEN SKATEBOARDS WILL BE FREE

1.

My FATHER BELIEVES THAT THE United States is destined one day to be engulfed in a socialist revolution. All revolutions are bloody, he says, but this one will be the bloodiest of them all. The working class—which includes me—will at some point in the not-so-distant future decide to put down the tools of our trade, pour into the streets, beat the police into submission, take over the means of production, and usher in a new epoch—the *final* epoch—of peace and equality. This revolution is not only inevitable, it is imminent. It is not only imminent, it is *quite* imminent. And when the time comes, my father will lead it.

Because of such urgency I do not see my father very often. This despite the fact we both live in New York City. Weeks pass. Months pass. Then a year. At times I will begin to wonder if I will ever hear from him again, but just as I do, a postcard will arrive from Istanbul, or Tehran, or Athens, or Minneapolis, where he has gone to attend this or that conference or to deliver this or that speech. "The weather is beautiful here," he will write in enormous swirling optimistic cursive that fills the white space, leaving room to say nothing more.

We've had our moments, though, over the years. My eighteenth birthday—the first time we had been together for any of my birthdays—my father astounded me by giving me a Walkman, by far the most expensive present I'd ever received. Then for my nineteenth birthday I stayed an entire week with him and his wife—his second wife—taking photographs, watching movies on the VCR, and playing Scrabble late into the night, where, even though my father is Iranian and English is his third language, he beat me nearly every time. We also took a long walk one Sunday afternoon, just him and me, to the aquarium at Coney Island, sitting side by side in the winter air while we watched as a walrus swam back and forth in its cement pond. Later at the café I was so nervous about being on my best behavior that I knocked over an entire cup of coffee onto his lap. "Sorry, Pop. Sorry. Sorry. Sorry." And every Sunday morning during my freshman year in college he would call to ask if he could help answer any questions I might be having with Algebra 101. He is a professor of mathematics, after all.

But first and foremost my father is a member—a *comrade*—of the Socialist Workers Party. He is a leading comrade, in fact, and has been for almost all my life. The responsibilities he chooses to undertake include, but are not limited to, editing books, writing articles, giving speeches, teaching political classes, attending book sales, demonstrations, rallies, meetings, conferences, picket lines . . . By the time I was in my early twenties my father had again begun to disappear behind this massive workload of revolution, and his phone calls grew increasingly infrequent until they ceased altogether, and our joyful reunions became more like occasional punctuation marks in long paragraphs of silence.

One summer night, when I was twenty-seven years old, I took my girlfriend to Film Forum in the West Village to watch a documentary on Che Guevara. When the movie was over, I came out of the theater to see my father standing on the sidewalk behind a table with an array of books published by Pathfinder Press, the publishing house of the Socialist Workers Party. *Che Guevara Speaks. Che Guevara Talks to Young People. The History of the Russian Revolution. Imperialism: The Highest Stage of Capitalism.* A handwritten banner was draped over the front of the table with a quote by Castro that read "There will be a victorious revolution in the United States before there will be a victorious counterrevolution in Cuba." In my father's hand, displayed for all to see, was that week's issue of *The Militant.*

"Sidsky!" my father called out, using his invented Russified diminutive of my name, which has never failed to endear him to me.

"Pop!" I said.

"How was the movie, Sidsky?"

"I liked it," I said.

And my girlfriend, who cared little for politics and had never even heard of Che Guevara before I had told her about him, said, "I liked it too."

"I see," my father said, looking first at my girlfriend and then at me. It was obvious by the expression on his face that we had given the wrong answer. I thought of backtracking and adding qualifications to my opinion, but before I could think what those qualifications could be, he said, "Let's have dinner tonight. What do you say? There's a nice restaurant right around the corner."

I agreed, of course, wholeheartedly. The only hitch was

that my father had to wait for the next showing of the documentary to let out, ninety minutes from now, and then he had to put all the unsold books away and fold up the table, so my girlfriend and I walked fourteen blocks through the West Village to my studio apartment to sit patiently by the phone, growing hungrier by the minute. And when my father finally called it was to say, sorry, a last-minute meeting had suddenly been scheduled, he could not see us tonight, but we would definitely do it again sometime soon, he promised, the three of us, soon.

"Oh, I can tell you're disappointed!" my girlfriend said, throwing her arms around me, kissing me.

"No, I'm not," I said, but I was.

And then the phone rang again, and it was my father again, but this time he was saying that the last-minute meeting had just been rescheduled, and, yes, he could have dinner now, right now, he was excited to see us, how soon could we be there? So my girlfriend and I hurried the fourteen blocks back through the Village to meet him at the nice restaurant around the corner from Film Forum, where we ate and drank our fill while he explained to us everything we had misunderstood about the movie.

Not long after that, I began to have feelings of claustrophobia around my girlfriend. We had been together for just one year, but all the excitement had worn away. I cringed at her affection. When she would ask if I had missed her after a few days apart, I would cruelly delight in telling her I had not. I broke up with her finally in front of Monet's *Water Lilies* at the Museum of Modern Art for what was supposed to be the beginning of a fun-filled weekend at her parents' house in upstate New York. And my father, almost about the same time, divorced his second wife of ten years. But while I remained single, unable to summon the courage to ask anyone out, sitting alone in the front row of Film Forum every weekend with regret, he had begun to date with gusto, beginning with a twenty-eight-year-old comrade from the party.

When I saw him next, it was in his new apartment in Brooklyn, shabby and unpainted, but I knew he didn't care. The apartment had a hollow, empty, unlived-in feel, like he was just moving in or just moving out. The reality was that he had already been there six months. There was hardly anything in the place except for a large desk in the living room littered with memorandums from the Socialist Workers Party. And next to the desk was a plant about to die. Next to the plant were two bookcases. One filled with forty-five volumes of the collected works of Lenin, including letters to relatives. And the second with forty-nine volumes of the collected works of Marx and Engels, also with letters to relatives. These had been given to him by his second wife one Christmas when times were still good. I remembered that Christmas. I had been there for it. Standing in the dim light next to the dying plant, I wondered if he had had the chance yet to read every volume. I wondered if I should read every volume.

My father abandoned me when I was nine months old, and with only a few exceptions I did not see or hear from him for eighteen years. "Mahmoud went off to fight for a world socialist revolution," my mother would tell me with proud determination when I was a little boy. *Mahmoud.* The name always sounded so ornate, so exotic, coming from my mother's mouth, and it emphasized the fact that my name was also exotic, while my mother was Martha Harris (née Finkelstein), a Jewish American, born and raised in the small town of Mount Vernon, New York. The divisons and allegiances, therefore, were various.

In any event, the logic behind my mother's explanation was that the separation with my father was only temporary and, once this socialist revolution had been achieved, he would return to us. It was only a matter of time. Neither of us ever dared state this belief aloud—it was unmarked and liquid—but we subscribed to it silently, like a well-kept secret among friends. And thus, since the night of my father's departure, she began to save herself for him, denying herself a sexual or even a personal life, never bothering to find either another husband for herself or a surrogate father for me. Indeed, she even consented to stay married to my father so that he could continue to live and work legally in the United States. Moreover, she remained a committed member of the Socialist Workers Party, pursuing the revolution with a ruthlessness and zeal that crushed whatever stood in her way. If the answer was revolution, then she would do everything in her power to make it solid.

And since there was something so immensely redemptive and exciting for me to imagine that my unknown father was not just a man who had abandoned me but a noble man of adventure who *had no choice* but to abandon me, I succumbed quite easily to my mother's version of events. This is but one example from the hagiography of my father that persisted throughout my childhood, that has persisted, in fact, until this very day.

But the story took great effort to sustain, and there were times when even my mother could not follow the narrative. "Mahmoud gave me twenty-four hours' notice before he left," she would confide on candid, reflective occasions. There would be an apologetic tone to her voice, one that implied regret at having to admit something so unsavory about such an important man. And while this was one of the only criticisms my mother ever levied against my father, it mirrored another theme that would define my childhood: my mother as a victim of the world, at the mercy of those more powerful than she, and by extension I was also at their mercy, as were each and every worker who was unfortunate enough to have been born under capitalism.

"The roots of suffering are in the capitalist system," she would explain. "We must do away with capitalism in order to do away with suffering." This meant that energy expended on eliminating the wretchedness of only one, when standing behind them were millions more in equal wretched need, was energy greatly wasted. There was even a story of how Lenin, during a devastating famine in the Volga region in which he lived as a young man, refused on principle to offer any aid to the sick and starving, even to those peasants of his own estate, reasoning that to alleviate their suffering would delay the coming revolution—which at that point was twenty-five years away.

My mother's philosophy, as callous and resolute as it might appear, was nonetheless underscored by a deep compassion that would come upon her quickly and from many directions. I would frequently see her cry about things like the general oppression of Palestinians, the heroic struggle of Castro against U.S. imperialism, the death of a young black boy at the hands of the police. "Did you hear what the police did to that boy?" she would say to me, her hands wringing the air, her body full of accusation as if I might be to blame. And then she would become incensed at the seemingly carefree disinterest of the wealthy. When we walked through a well-to-do neighborhood, she would point to a large house with smoke in the chimney and a car in the driveway and say contemptuously, "Look at them. The rich asses." And I would look at that house and I would despise the occupants for having, and I would despise myself for not having, and further down, much further down, I would despise myself for wanting what I saw.

We were poor, my mother and I, living in a world of doom and gloom, pessimism and bitterness, where storms raged and wolves scratched at the door. Often she would inform me when we were late on the rent, or when she suspected she was about to be fired, or when the price of bread had gone up again. All of it categorical evidence against capitalism and how deserving we would be when the revolution came. At times our deprivation entered the realm of the absurd. Like when she would stand at the entrance of the supermarket, asking shoppers if they would give her the classifieds from their newspapers. Or at the doctor's office, filling her knapsack with towelettes. Or in front of the library, instructing me to go and place our overdue books on the counter and walk straight back outside. Later she would brag to comrades about what a good accomplice I had been. And if I ever questioned such dishonesty, she would reply, "Any crime against society is a good crime."

On one occasion I mustered the courage to ask my mother to buy me a skateboard (they were all the rage at the time), and after much inveigling she finally agreed to have a look. There in the middle of the sports department sat a giant metal bin filled with skateboards in bubblegum-bright colors and a sign that read *$10.99.*

"I want the green one," I said.

"Once the revolution comes," my mother said, "everyone will have a skateboard, because all skateboards will be free." Then she took me by the hand and led me out of the store. I pictured in precise detail a world of long, rolling, grassy hills, where it was always summertime and boys skateboarded up and down the slopes.

2

WHEN I WAS FOUR YEARS old there arose one morning an unresolvable crisis between my mother and me.

I was in my bedroom playing with my toys when she entered and knelt beside me on the floor. "We will not be eating grapes or lettuce anymore," she said plainly.

I put my toys down and looked up into her face. It seemed odd and outlandish, this sudden rule. The kind of rule that comes from nowhere, out of nowhere, made solely at the whim of the adult world.

"That's a dumb rule," I said.

"It's not a dumb rule," she said. And she went on to patiently explain that the rule was not her own but the rule of the Socialist Workers Party, which was itself following the rule of César Chávez and the United Farm Workers, who had called for a national boycott of table grapes and iceberg lettuce. All of this she described in the simplest of terms that allowed me to understand and accept the edict.

"You're such a good boy," she said, and she kissed me on the top of my head.

As the days passed, however, and the boycott carried on, I found that my desire for grapes began to eclipse my compassion for the workers. Now it was my turn to interrupt my mother one morning.

"I'm ready to eat grapes," I said. I said it as plainly as she had.

She closed the book she was reading and looked down at me quizzically. "You can't eat grapes," she said. "You know that." And then she added, "And you can't eat iceberg lettuce."

"I don't want to eat iceberg lettuce," I responded brightly, thinking that she would see this as a welcome compromise.

"Well, you can't eat that either," she said with measure. Adult with child, adult instructing child. I detected, though, somewhere beneath her rational exterior, an undercurrent of satisfaction.

"I want to eat grapes," I said.

"You can't eat grapes," she said.

And then I screamed: "I want to eat grapes! I want to eat grapes!" And I melted to the floor, rolling onto my back. "I want to eat grapes! I want to eat grapes!"

"Well, you can't eat grapes," the light and airy voice said, "and you can't eat iceberg lettuce."

From there on, the absence of grapes became a constant, unyielding presence in my life. It seemed I was never far from a political poster about not eating grapes, or a leaflet, or a T-shirt, or a conversation, or a forum. I descended into a state of perpetual yearning that intertwined so tightly with my desire that it soon became impossible to distinguish one from the other and that established a terrible equation for me. Desire = yearning.

All of this culminated in the button my mother made me pin to my jacket, which featured the logo of the United Farm Workers—a black eagle with wings spread wide against a blood-red background—along with the unequivocal imperative, *Don't Eat Grapes.* I interpreted this not so much as an entreaty to the outside world as a scarlet letter to remind me of my own sinful desire, which, if ever quenched, would be through the immiseration of others.

"Is the boycott over yet?" I'd ask my mother.

"Not yet," she'd say.

"When will the boycott be over?"

"When the capitalists give the workers their rights."

"When will that happen?"

"I don't know."

"When it happens, will we eat grapes?"

"Yes."

Weeks passed.

"Is the boycott over?"

"No."

Months passed.

"Is the boycott over?"

"No."

Fall came. Then winter. Grapes were no longer in season.

"Is the boycott over?"

"No."

I had become that fox I had learned about in Aesop's fable who jumped again and again without success at the bunch of grapes dangling on the branch above him. The story that the fox concocts in order to soothe himself and allay his disappointment is that the grapes themselves are most likely sour and not, in the end, worth his trouble. The conclusion I drew, however, was of a different nature. I began to see what my mother saw: The flaw was inside me. Desire under capitalism—*all* desire—was a shameful, unwanted condition, and one should never attempt to satisfy that desire but instead, through heightened consciousness of the world, transcend it and by so doing rid oneself of it forever.

Three blocks from our apartment in Brooklyn was the supermarket in which my mother and I would do our weekly shopping. This occasion presented a predicament for the two of us. Not only was I in close proximity to great mountains of grapes but I was also keenly aware that my neighbors, many of them black, most of them poor, would effortlessly and without any apparent compunction load up their shopping carts with the fruit.

"Look, Ma," I'd say, "it's okay for us to eat grapes."

"No, it's not."

And once we had completed our shopping, I would have to stand beside her in front of the supermarket while she unzipped her knapsack and handed out an endless supply of leaflets with the black eagle, the red background, the three simple words.

Then one day, after untold months of my ceaseless and unending demand, we were standing in the middle of the produce aisle when she said to me with obvious exasperation, "Eat one grape!"

I could not believe my good fortune. Immediately I reached my hand up toward the piles towering above me and I plucked without choosing. The grape was heavier than I remembered grapes to be. I popped it into my mouth and bit down; fluid squirted into my cheeks. I chewed happily, violating the farm workers without remorse. Then three things occurred all at once. The first was that I realized how delicious the grape was, vindication of all the effort I had expended on obtaining it. The second was that I resolved this would not be the last time I was ever permitted to eat a grape. Finally, and most essential, I understood that the simple act of eating instantly rewrote the formula between desire and yearning, creating a new equation: desire + yearning = theft.

What was paramount for my mother, though, was that I had not breached the sanctity of the boycott. If anything, the supermarket took a loss on their investment and therefore, in an indirect way, thievery actually strengthened the struggle of the farm workers. Desire + yearning + theft = revolution.

The next time we were in the grocery store, my mother, now unable to turn back from the course of her decision, again allowed me to have a grape. The next time I ate without permission. "I'm just having one, Ma," but I had two. After that, I ate three. So on and so forth. It became so habitual that I would stand leisurely in front of the mounds of grapes as if they were a buffet and I was considering my options. I would pluck casually as my mother shopped elsewhere in the store, my button informing the world to do the opposite of what I was doing.

One afternoon, in the midst of my revelry, with my mouth full and my hand reaching, I had the uncomfortable sensation that I was being observed. Not too far away, an elderly white woman was staring at me intently. I resented her interference in what I had come to think of as a private moment, and I stopped chewing.

"Go ahead," she said sweetly. "Go ahead and eat another one."

I wanted to follow her suggestion, but there was something in her voice that made me hesitate. Were her words really words of encouragement? I sensed that I was in danger of being entrapped by the indecipherable language of adult sarcasm. I peered at the woman, who in turn peered at me. She had snow-white hair and leaned heavily on a cane and did not appear to have an unkind face. Perhaps she supported the boycott and therefore saw me as an ally championing the rights of migrant workers. It struck me suddenly how peculiar it was that an adult would actually endorse thievery, and I somehow sensed that I was following a peculiar set of rules. They were, of course, the correct rules, but they had set me in opposition to the rest of the world, where my right was everyone else's wrong, and where my wrong was everyone else's right, and where I would be helpless in ever being able to distinguish for myself which one was which.

On a warm summer day, one year after the boycott had begun and with no resolution in sight, my mother took me into Manhattan to visit the Empire State Building. The excursion had been planned weeks in advance, and my next-door neighbor and best friend, Britton, had been invited to come along as well. I had looked forward to the trip with such eagerness that when we finally surfaced from the subway station at Forty-second Street, I instantly spotted the tower, its antenna stretching into the clouds, and I screamed at Britton at the top of my lungs, "Look at that, will you!"

It was lunchtime, and so the three of us walked into Bryant Park directly behind the library to eat a snack before embarking for our destination. In the early seventies, Bryant Park was not the beautiful deep-green urban oasis that it has since become. It was a neglected patch of diseased and pock-marked grass, enclosed by a stark iron fence and enormous hedges and frequented by drug dealers and drug users, prostitutes and beggars. The three of us found a seat on a bench near the statue of the poet William Cullen Bryant, his face grave and paternal as he watched out over the unhappy state of his park. Britton sat across from me, his lunch bag on his lap, his legs swinging to and fro. He was a year older than me, tall, slim, black, the son of sharecroppers who spoke with Southern accents. I would often squander entire days in his bedroom, lolling about on the floor as we watched cartoons until his mom or dad said it was time for me to go home.

"Eat your lunch," my mother said to us.

Britton and I began to extract the food, one by one, that our respective mothers had packed for us in our brown paper bags. When I withdrew my bag of carrot sticks, I could not help but notice that Britton withdrew a fat and yellow Twinkie. I watched as he unwrapped it slowly, as if it might be a birthday present, and then devoured it bite by bite, each bite cautious and calculated, until there was nothing left except to lick the cream from his fingers.

"Eat your carrots," my mother said.

I stuffed them into my mouth and chewed without tasting.

"Don't eat so fast," she said.

I ignored her: chewed, swallowed, burped, and then stuck my hand back into the paper bag like a gambler thinking that his luck is about to change. Instead, I pulled out a container of yogurt. I looked up in time to see Britton holding a small bag of cookies. Was there nothing but treats in his bag?

"I don't want my yogurt," I announced boldly.

"Then eat your crackers."

The word *crackers* struck me heavily. I felt humiliated by the word.

"I'm not hungry," I said.

"Well, you're going to be hungry."

"I don't want my crackers!" My voice was loud enough to catch Britton's attention and make him pause mid-bite. He looked at me curiously before he began chewing. Brown crumbs fell. Pigeons approached.

I handed my lunch to my mother. "I'm done eating."

"You're going to be hungry," she said again, but I had no interest in foresight.

"Let's go," I said grandly. "I'm ready to go to the Empire State Building."

"But Britton isn't finished eating yet."

I wheeled toward him. "It's time to go!"

But he ignored me and sunk his arm deep into the

bottomless paper bag, feeling around to see what other goodies there might be. And then he withdrew, like a surgeon performing a delicate operation, an enormous bunch of grapes.

I stared in horror.

"Britton isn't finished eating yet," I heard my mother repeat in the background.

The grapes were green and shiny and they glistened with moisture, every one, and I was sure they had been purchased from the same supermarket in which my mother and I shopped. Britton cradled them in his hand and then lifted them up by their stem, as if he wished to display them to everyone in the park. Then he selected one, the plumpest one of them all, and ate it.

"Hey, you," I said. "You shouldn't be eating those."

Britton looked at me, mystified. "What?"

"You shouldn't be eating those!" My voice was shrill, my finger pointing in accusation. I stood up from the bench and took a step toward him, thinking that I would snatch the grapes and smash them against the concrete. My mother would applaud my action.

"Ma!" I said. But when I turned to her for assistance, she was gazing at me with a befuddled look.

"What?" she said.

What? Where had her outrage gone? I was swirling in bright lights of confusion. Britton laughed.

"Don't laugh!" I said, whipping around to him.

"I didn't laugh," he said.

Then my mother laughed, but when I whirled back to her, she had stopped. A crazy man tossed a handful of bread crumbs into the air and cried out in delight, "Whee! Whee!"

I turned and hurried through the pigeons, which rose above me in agitation. At the edge of the park I could see cars speeding by in all directions. I waited to hear my mother call for me to return—"Saïd! Saïd!"—but she did not. When I looked back, I saw that she was still sitting on the bench, watching me dispassionately. The bunch of grapes remained in Britton's hand, but he had stopped chewing. I walked to the corner, slowly enough so that I would be able to hear my mother's voice. The light was red, and I waited for it to turn green and then I waited for it to turn red again. Then I remembered that we had come all the way from Brooklyn to see the Empire State Building. The thought startled me into the present and filled me with something like hope, and I turned back to my mother, but when I did it was as if I had stepped into the rabbit hole and the park was gone. I turned again. Was I facing the way I had come or the way I had gone? I ventured from the curb and a car horn boomed loudly, sending me scrambling back to the sidewalk. I could no longer see the Empire State Building; it had been swallowed by the faces of adults who loomed above, a sea of faces, each one hideous and unfamiliar.

"Is there something wrong with the boy?"

"Is the boy lost?"

"What's your name, honey?"

"I think he's lost."

"Are you lost, honey?"

The faces of elderly women surrounded me, looking

down with smiles. A police car drew up to the curb, its lights flashing red, and a door opened and I was escorted into the backseat.

"Don't worry, son," one of the officers said to me. "We'll find your mother and father." He smiled at me. "What's your name, son?"

I told the officer my name. The name was repeated into the radio. The radio responded. The police car pulled away from the curb and into snarled traffic. And all of a sudden, from out of the bubbling cauldron of the city, a shirtless old man appeared, thin and drunk, rapping urgently on the window.

"Officer! Officer!" the man cried breathlessly.

The officers ignored him and inched the car forward.

"Officer! Officer!" *Rap rap rap.*

With a casual air, one of the officers unrolled his window. "How can we help you today, sir?"

"Officer," the man implored, "there are men in the park hitting me with sticks."

I felt alarm, but the officer showed no concern. "Can't you see we have a lost little boy here?" he said.

The thin man absorbed me with his pink eyes and then quickly returned to the officers. "Officer, they're hitting me—"

"There's an officer on duty in the park," the officer said. "He'll handle the matter for you."

"Please!" the man said, but the traffic was unclogged now and the officer was rolling his window up, muting the sounds of the city. The old man's voice faded away. And I sank comfortably into the cushions of the backseat, thinking that I could sit there forever, happy within the insulated bubble of the police car with the world floating harmlessly by. I knew, also, that this was the wrong thought to be having. "The police are bad," my mother had told me many times. "They are not part of the working class. They help the bosses to oppress." I had also been haunted by a photo that seemed to run nearly every week in *The Militant,* showing a young black boy being choked by an enormous white New York City police officer. Suddenly I realized that my mother had dressed me that day in a big blue T-shirt supporting the Equal Rights Amendment. I was positive this T-shirt would be seen as an affront by the police officers, and I curled into myself in the backseat to make it less conspicuous. Through the window I could see the top of the Empire State Building come into view, its antenna still in the clouds, then we rounded a corner and it was gone.

At the police station I sat on a plastic chair beside filing cabinets. The officers who had found me joined with other officers in discussing my situation. I waited patiently and with my arms folded. Soon a very large officer—larger than all the rest—took me by the hand and led me down a hallway and into another room, which was empty except for a vending machine. We stood in front of the machine together, he and I and my T-shirt.

"Which kind do you like?" he said.

Rows of ice cream spread out in front of me.

"Nothing, mister," I said.

"Come on," he said, "what's your favorite flavor?"

"Chocolate, mister." It seemed a painful admission.

"I knew it," he said, and he reached into his pocket and took out some coins and dropped them into the machine. I listened to them clink. Then he pulled the lever and out came a chocolate ice cream sandwich. He gave it to me.

"Thank you, mister."

Then he put his hand in mine and led me back to the plastic chair, where my mother and Britton sat waiting.

We did not embrace when we saw each other. My mother told me that because of this unexpected, inconsiderate diversion, we had run out of time to visit the Empire State Building and would now return home straightaway. There was still paperwork to fill out and things to sign, and the three of us sat on our plastic chairs, staring ahead wordlessly. After a while, Britton produced a small rubber ball from his pocket and proceeded to bounce it up and down in front of him.

"I don't think it's a good idea to bounce that in here," my mother said. She said it quietly, like she was passing a secret from one person to the next. Did she mean that he shouldn't bounce the ball because black boys who bounced balls in police stations would have their heads split open? An officer came by with a pen and paper, and my mother stood and conferred with him. Then another officer came by. Britton swung his legs casually in front of him. One, two, three. One, two, three. The ice cream lay in my lap. It was growing soft and warm. I could see that it was quickly melting and beginning to ooze against its wrapper. Soon it would become nothing but chocolate liquid. If I was going to eat it, I had to eat it now.

"Are you going to eat that?" Britton asked.

"Yes," I said.

"When?"

"Soon."

He went back to swinging his legs. One, two, three. I looked at the ice cream in my lap. I did not unwrap it.

3

I'VE JUST WALKED OUT OF a coffee shop at Union Square to see a Socialist Workers Party book table set up on the corner. "Olga Rodríguez for Mayor. Vote Socialist Workers," the banner reads, because it's October 1997 and everybody in the city is gearing up for the forthcoming mayoral election between Rudy Giuliani and Ruth Messinger. Everybody but me, that is. I've never voted in any election—mayoral, presidential, or otherwise—and I don't intend to do so now. To cast my ballot for Olga Rodríguez would be to bend to my father's will; to cast my ballot for someone else would be to betray him.

There are a half dozen comrades standing in front of the table, holding out that week's *Militant* to the people walking past. It's Saturday, and the streets are teeming with NYU students, and couples out for a stroll, and boys with basketballs, but no one stops.

"End police brutality. Defend immigrant rights. Vote for a working-class alternative," one of the men says to a group of young black women carrying violin cases. They walk on as if they've heard nothing. The comrade follows after them for a moment and then retreats. His hair is bushy and uncombed and his shoes are scuffed. He is young but looks old. An enormous knapsack hangs off his back.

Maybe I should buy a copy of *The Militant* from him.

Why not? It's only $1.50. Plus if my father shows up he'll be delighted. "Sidsky! Let's have lunch!"

I spent my Saturdays as a little boy playing on the sidewalk next to these book tables, hoping that someone would stop to buy. The locations varied from week to week; sometimes it was in front of a supermarket or a school or a public library, sometimes on the sidelines of a demonstration, sometimes just a corner on a crowded street. Sometimes it was in the rain and sometimes the dead of winter. I can still hear my mother's voice, slight but grave, as she repeated the week's headline over and over like a mantra, hoping to interest passersby in purchasing that issue, or in purchasing an entire subscription, or in purchasing a book. Or in joining the party.

"End U.S. imperialist domination of the Middle East," she might say one hundred times on a Saturday, five hundred times, a thousand times.

From my place on the sidewalk I would look up and watch her every so often. When a person neared, she would take a few quick steps toward them with *The Militant* outstretched, her body language such that it seemed as if she was considering taking a stroll with that person, and the person, acutely aware of her proximity, would stiffen and quicken their pace, leaving my mother behind. The whole interaction took only seconds. She had at most ten words to make her pitch.

"End U.S. imperialist domination of . . ."

"End U.S. . . ."

As the strangers approached, one after the other, I would will them to buy *The Militant* from my mother. Maybe this person is going to, I would think. Maybe that other person is going to. I willed a thousand *Militant*s to be bought, ten thousand, one million. And for every thousand people who hurried past without stopping, there would be that one who, like a miracle, would stop to discuss, or to buy, or to put their name on a mailing list to receive announcements about upcoming events. And for every million, there would be the one who would actually join the party.

But whatever happened that Saturday, whatever contribution big or small—maybe just a car honking in support— would be enough to give my mother the sustenance to show up the next weekend to do it all over again.

It was a table just like this table that my parents passed by one autumn afternoon in 1964 on the campus of the University of Minnesota and stopped for a moment, only a moment, to listen to what it was all about.

They had met each other by chance seven years earlier at a dinner party hosted by a mutual friend. My mother was an aspiring novelist studying for an undergraduate degree in English literature, and my father was working toward a doctorate in mathematics. His journey from Tehran to Minneapolis was a long and improbable one that began when he was eighteen years old and had entered an essay contest on the theme "What is liberty?" The contest had been sponsored by the U.S. government, and offered, as grand prize, a scholarship to study at an American university. The irony that my father would hold forth eloquently enough on the subject of liberty to win the scholarship and then spend the rest of his life trying to overthrow the very government that had provided him with that scholarship is trumped by the irony that the government that had asked him to consider the idea of liberty was itself plotting to overthrow the prime minister of Iran, Mohammed Mossadegh. My father has recounted that on the night of that coup in 1953, he gathered in the darkened streets of Tehran with a group of other young men his age, all of them trying to figure out what, if anything, they could do to help their country. When the Shah's tanks rolled past, they realized there was nothing they could do, and so they went back inside their homes and locked the doors, and a few weeks later my father was happily, thankfully, learning math in the United States.

My mother, on the other hand, had chosen the University of Minnesota because her brother was there studying for his doctorate. It had been an easy decision for her to make, as her brother was Mark Harris, already an accomplished novelist who would go on to write nearly twenty books, most famously *Bang the Drum Slowly,* which was turned into a film starring Robert De Niro. My mother did not arrive at the university alone, however, but with her own mother, who was crippled from rheumatoid arthritis and confined to a wheelchair. Her mother had been a frail, infirm woman nearly all her life, suffering from one debilitating illness after another. And her father had been the opposite: a lawyer and landlord, stormy and contentious at both, who allowed his New York City apartment buildings to fall into disrepair, suing and countersuing tenants with verve until he was eventually disbarred for having swindled a business partner. When my mother was four years old, her mother contracted rheumatic fever—for the second time—and during her struggle to regain her health her husband proposed she go to Clearwater, Florida, for six months while he remained behind. This was just the first of many times that my mother's father would devise a way to separate from the family under dubious pretenses. Lonely, bewildered, and unable to properly care for her children in a strange city, my ailing grandmother made the decision to place my mother into first grade at the age of four. It was a decision from which my mother would never recover: held back in fifth grade, put on probation in college, and constantly shadowed by her own sense that she was intellectually deficient. "Martha seems immature for her age," her first-grade teacher wrote home on her report card, apparently not taking into account that the little girl was nearly two years younger than her classmates. When her father abandoned the family once and for all eight years later, disappearing into Manhattan forever, he left behind his twelve-year-old daughter (both sons were already grown and gone) to care for a wife who was on the verge of becoming an invalid. Before leaving for school in the morning, my mother would dress her mother, comb her hair, and tie her shoes. And each night, without fail, she would wake and pad into her mother's bedroom, where she would slip her arms under the wasted body racked with pain—sixteen aspirin a day— and turn her from one side to the other. But by the time my mother was nineteen and a sophomore in college, she had managed to extricate herself from her mother, sending her on a train back to Mount Vernon to be cared for by others.

So at that dinner party in 1957, the young Jewish woman

and the young Iranian man were introduced for the first time, and saw something in each other, and fell in love, and about one year later they were married, and one year after that they had a son named Jacob, and three years after that a daughter named Jamileh.

By the early 1960s the Minneapolis area had become one of the most successful recruiting hubs for the Socialist Workers Party. The "cradle of the movement" it was called, an immodest nod to St. Petersburg, which had been christened "cradle of the revolution" by the Bolsheviks. Groups of young comrades—*trailblazers*—would travel around the region, going from campus to campus as they tried to win students over to the idea of socialism. It was at the University of Minnesota where a half dozen of these comrades happened to arrive one Saturday morning in 1964, and unfold their book table, laid out their *Militant*s, and draped their banner that proclaimed "Clifton DeBerry for President. Vote Socialist Workers."

I can picture those half dozen comrades standing there in much the same way as these half dozen comrades stand now on the corner at Union Square. I can picture the same exhausted diligence, the same knapsacks, the same scuffed shoes, the same *Militant*. Except then it cost ten cents.

"Why U.S. is losing war against Vietnam rebels!"

"Washington admits arming Congo mercenaries!"

"Cops in New York kill another Puerto Rican!"

Over and over I am sure they called, until it was

afternoon and their mouths were dry and they decided that the time had come to call it a day. And just as they were beginning to pack up their books and roll up their banner for Clifton DeBerry, I can see a young couple passing by with two strollers as they enjoyed the final days of autumn.

"Let's give it one last try," one of the comrades says, approaching the young couple with *Militant* in hand. "Read why Johnson is no answer to Goldwater."

The couple stops.

"We say it is only through the overthrow of capitalism that inequalities in society can be resolved."

"How much?" the couple ask.

"Ten cents," he says.

And the young wife reaches into her purse, because back then she carried a purse instead of a knapsack, and she wore dresses and high heels and lipstick, and kept her hair long, and showed off her legs to their best advantage.

"Thank you," says the comrade, pocketing the dime and handing them *The Militant*. Then the three of them chat for a while, a second comrade joining in, maybe a third. I am sure they were all friendly people, these comrades, friendly and vivacious and young and full of ideas.

"Will you vote for Clifton DeBerry in November?"

"He's the first black man to ever run for president."

"Here's a pamphlet of what he says about the working class."

"I would vote for him," says the young Iranian man, "but I'm not a citizen." (Nor will he ever be.)

And this proscription on voting will enrage the comrades,

who see it as yet another form of discrimination against immigrants.

"Do you see?" they say. "Do you see?"

The young woman, however, accepts the pamphlet on Clifton DeBerry and says that she will consider voting for him. Then one of the children begins to grow restless and the couple begs their leave of the comrades, thanks them for their time, for their newspaper, for their ideas. And at the last possible second, one of the young comrades suggests: "Would you like to join our mailing list?"

"We'll help to keep you informed."

"There are many upcoming events."

"There's no obligation, of course."

So the couple fill out their names and phone number and then say good-bye to the comrades.

Later that night, I can see them lying side by side in bed in their college housing after the children have fallen asleep, looking through *The Militant* together. Maybe there is a reprint of the speech that James Baldwin gave during a rent strike in Harlem. This will appeal to the English literature major. Maybe there is a photograph of the Shah standing next to a grinning Lyndon Johnson, with the caption "The Blood-stained Shah." And this will appeal to the young man who watched the tanks roll past his doorstep. Or there is an article about Che. Or about Patrice Lumumba. Or about Vietnam. Or about Trotsky. There is an excitement to the paper that the couple can feel, lying next to each other, toes touching, a sense that all the big things that are taking place in the world are connected to this paper, are influenced by it.

There is also a sadness to the paper as it lays out in unflinching detail the misery of the world. But this sadness is offset by hope: Things can change, of course they can change. And beneath the excitement, beneath the sadness, beneath the hope, lies revenge, its tentacles coiling around the reader. I am sure they felt this too.

Maybe it is a week later when a comrade calls and invites them to attend a forum on Cuba or Vietnam. The husband discusses it with his wife, who agrees that they will cancel their plans for that Friday evening and she will stay home and watch the four-year-old and the one-year-old while he goes off. Then a few weeks later there is another invitation to another forum, but this time the wife goes along and the children are left in the care of neighbors.

"We'll be home by eleven."

"Take your time."

At the forum the young woman is swayed by the certainty, the confidence of the speakers, and she removes a few more precious coins from her purse and buys a subscription to *The Militant*. When November arrives she ignores what the multitudes are saying about Johnson being better than Goldwater, and makes up her own mind, pulling the lever for Clifton DeBerry. (He received thirty-two thousand votes.) After that, Malcolm X is assassinated and the Vietnam War accelerates and the subscription is renewed and the husband decides that New York City is the place to be for revolutionary action. So the two of them pack all their things, and along with their son and daughter they leave the campus of the University of Minnesota for an apartment in

Brooklyn. Now there are more forums, more books, more demonstrations, and the young woman's dream of being a writer is pushed aside for the work that is the greater work, the greater dream, until there is no room left for anything else. And Che is assassinated, and Martin Luther King is assassinated, and Nixon is elected (she cast her ballot for Fred Halstead—forty-one thousand votes), and after that a third child is born—which is me—and meanwhile the Vietnam War continues, the demonstrations grow more violent, and the meetings more frequent. On and on the husband and wife go, further and further, faster and faster, until one day there is a pause, briefly, and the husband stands at the front door of their apartment, his hand on the doorknob, looking down and away from his wife and three children, a sheepish look on his face and an overnight bag in his hand. Then he opens the door and tiptoes out quietly into that good night forever.

4

THROUGH THE MILKY DARKNESS I crawled, imagining I was swimming my way through the ocean. Over the seats I went, from lap to lap. The laps were boats.

"How's the little revolutionary tonight?" a voice whispered in my ear.

I couldn't see the face with the voice.

"I'm good," I whispered back.

Then passing headlights illuminated everything briefly, red, yellow, blue, blinking, blinking, and I could see the inside of the Greyhound bus, the narrow aisle, the bags overhead, and the comrade smiling down at me. Then it all went back to black. I moved on, my six-year-old body swerving as the bus swerved, the sound of the motor humming beneath me, making me drowsy. "What's the little revolutionary doing?" the voices asked. "Where's the little revolutionary going?"

When I awoke, it was morning and all had been transformed. The noise, the dirt, the large buildings of New York City were gone. Everything had become very wide and very flat. The sidewalks looked like they had been scrubbed in anticipation of our arrival, and when I stepped from the bus my mother bent down to untie my shoes so I could walk barefoot. There were no clouds in the sky, and the sunshine beat down. The air smelled fresh. I was now on the campus of Oberlin College in Oberlin, Ohio, where the Socialist Workers Party held its annual national convention. For one week every August, a thousand comrades from all over the country, and some from overseas, even, gathered here to elect committees, discuss strategy, attend political classes, and raise funds.

Under the trees I went running.

"Where are you, Saïd?" my mother called. "Come help me with the luggage."

And the two of us stood over our suitcases, trying to right them, trying to pull them, until a comrade said, "It's okay, Martha, I'll get those for you." And my mother and I walked gratefully behind him to the dormitory we had been assigned to live in for the week. A small, clean, square room, with two beds and a wooden desk that faced out over the wide grassy lawn. "Look at me, Ma!" I said, leaping from one bed to the other. "Look at me, I'm Superman!" From the window I could see the crab apple trees that the year before I had climbed and gorged so much from that I had diarrhea for two days. On top of our dresser a stack of towels and an orange bar of soap had been generously provided for us. "The soap smells good, Ma!"

After we had unpacked, my mother took a nap while I went out to explore the dormitory. Through the hallways I scampered, and up and down the staircases, marveling at the alternating sensations of carpeting and linoleum on my bare feet, while feeling as if I had once again become the proprietor of an enormous hotel in which everything belonged to me. I darted in and out of the lounges, where the comrades had gathered to smoke and discuss, and through the lobby, where the giant banners were being hung about the Vietnam War and the Fourth International and the Equal Rights Amendment.

"There goes the little revolutionary!" they yelled as I passed.

Just one flight below my dorm room was the cafeteria, and later that afternoon my mother and I walked down the stairs for lunch, greeting the other comrades who had just arrived from Chicago and Detroit and Los Angeles, with hundreds more still on their way. "Martha," the comrades said, "I haven't seen you since . . ." "Saïd," they said, "look how tall you're getting!"

In the cafeteria I was permitted to eat and drink without fear of reprisal. No accusation was ever leveled by my mother when I returned to the table with yet another tray piled with plates of French fries and pizza and cake and cookies. It was the chocolate milk that I loved the most and consumed in vast quantities. I found it incomprehensible that it could flow so uninterruptedly from the soda fountain. My mother explained to me that the milk was not free, that none of the food was in fact free, and that she had paid a onetime fee for everything, but since I did not see money change hands I felt as if all was free. And it was here at Oberlin that I began to draw a strong association between revolution and summertime and grassy fields and all-you-can-eat.

That evening, as dusk began to fall, my mother and I walked to the skating rink on the other end of campus, where the first meeting of the convention was always held. I sat beside her on a folding chair while comrades filed in, filling the place, their voices bouncing off the round bubble of the rink so that a thousand people sounded like a million. From out of this crowd I could hear the faint calling of my name.

"Saïd!"

The voices were far off but coming closer.

"Saïd!"

I stood on my chair and strained to locate their origin.

"Saïd!"

And suddenly, out of the crush of comrades, two small comrades emerged, brown eyes and brown hair, bearing an odd and unlikely resemblance to me: my brother and sister.

"There you are!" they shouted.

I was shocked by how much taller they had grown since the last time I had seen them. And my sister's hair was long now, like a woman's, and my brother was showing the signs of a mustache. They each wore little buttons on their collars that said *Join the YSA,* because they were members of the youth wing of the party, the Young Socialist Alliance. I suddenly felt shy in front of them, and I flinched when they touched me.

"I caught a fish!" my brother exclaimed, bending down and picking me up into his arms.

"Should we fry the fish tonight?" my sister asked.

"No, no, no," I squealed, and in this way I was coaxed into laughter.

And then my mother came over. "Hello, Jacob," she said with a stiff formality, extending her hand for him to shake.

Some of the comrades offered to slide down so we could all sit in a row, and when we were settled in, my brother and sister told me which dormitory they were staying in, and they told me a funny story about unpacking, and they told me that my father was somewhere in the front of the audience, or in the middle of the audience, and that he wanted to see me, but he couldn't see me just yet because he was discussing things with the speakers, but soon enough. Then they asked me what funny things I'd been doing the last six months, or the last year, or however long it had been since we had seen one another, but before I could tell them, a speaker took the stage, a hush descended over the skating rink, and my brother and sister took out their notebooks and pens.

"Welcome, comrades," the comrade said into the microphone, his voice echoing. And so the speeches began.

There had been a time in the beginning when we had all been together. Five of us. But things did not go well, and about three years after my father left, my sister was packed up and sent off to a mysterious neighborhood in Brooklyn where my father was said to be living with a female comrade from the party. I retained a single memory of my sister, from when she was probably eight and I was probably three, and she was kneeling in front of me to take off my shoes, but, unable to figure out how to undo the knot, what was supposed to be untied became tied tighter. And the two of us laughed and laughed.

In her absence, my brother and I filled the apartment with elaborate games. He was twelve years old, and so I was more than happy to parade behind him as his second-in-command. "Our bedroom is the jungle," he would say, "and our beds are lions." Or he would say, "I'm Superman and you're Batman." But just a few months after my sister left, my brother was also packed up and sent away, leaving me with a final image of him digging his hand into a cereal box and withdrawing a free prize, a plastic yellow dinosaur, which he graciously handed over to me.

So by the time I was four years old it was just my mother and me. And I became friends with Britton, spending my days in his bedroom, lolling about, watching cartoons.

Then one day my sister magically returned to us, just like that, saying she had been unhappy with my father, saying she didn't like his girlfriend, and giving me the impression that things had reversed themselves and soon my brother would return as well. The single memory of my sister trying to untie my shoelaces now became many memories. There we are in the morning, walking to school together. There we are in the afternoon, returning home. There we are at night, my sister tucking me into bed, kissing me, and then, inexplicably, plucking a single hair from her head, which I place inside my security blanket so it tickles my face as I sleep.

One afternoon while playing outside in the playground, I tumbled from my tricycle and was knocked unconscious. When I awoke from my daze, my sister was sitting beside me.

"It's going to be okay," she said, and she bent down and picked up me in one arm and my tricycle in the other.

At the entrance to our building, a strange man saw the dilemma and came to our aid. "Let me carry your brother," he offered.

"No," my sister said, "*I'll* carry my brother. *You* carry the tricycle."

Shortly after that incident, she went to visit my father for the weekend and upon her return to us made a careless remark about what a good time she had had. My mother abruptly flew into a rage. "Which one of us do you want to live with?" she screamed from across the dinner table.

"I want to live with you, Ma!"

"Decide tonight! Once and for all!"

"I said I want to live with you, Ma!"

My mother's fury escalated and then raged on like a storm. I followed along, watching from the outskirts, as it moved from room to room. My sister stayed silent throughout, her face an expression of blankness. An hour into the ordeal, my mother, in order to emphasize a point she was making, picked up a dozen of my sister's coloring markers that were near at hand and flung them across the room. They skidded over the floor and under the furniture, each and every one in its own direction. Instantly I fell to my hands and knees and set about retrieving them, happy to work toward a fruitful end. When I had gathered them all up, I presented them to my sister. Even in the midst of my mother's rampage, she had the presence of mind to turn and thank me.

"Thank you," she said.

"You're welcome," I said.

"Decide! Decide!"

Later that night, near midnight, in the quiet of the apartment, I watched from the bedroom doorway as my sister packed a small bag of her belongings.

"Will you be coming back again?" I asked her.

"No," she said. And she never did.

During the long days at Oberlin while everyone, including my brother and sister, was sequestered behind closed doors for their meetings and plenums, I passed the time by playing with the other dozen or so children of comrades. My favorite was Frankie Halstead, son of Fred Halstead—a leading member of the party, presidential candidate in 1968, and something like four hundred pounds. Frankie was just a few years older than me, and he was not so big as his father; in fact, he was short and skinny, but he carried himself with an outsize bravado that I admired. Once I had watched him argue with a pompous thirteen-year-old from the Young Socialist Alliance and then resolve it by pushing him clear over the hedges. He was also excellent at baseball and seemed to have every statistic committed to memory. He had baseball cards, and baseball programs, and a foul ball that he had caught at a Dodger game. "You can have it," he told me, "I catch thirty of them a year."

With Frankie in the lead, us dozen children would move like cattle over the campus, going from one grassy lawn to the next, discovering new things as we went, until the entire campus had been traversed. Everything was silent and still. No adult was ever sighted. We frolicked unobserved. "Let's go climb the tree behind the library," Frankie might suggest, and off we would go. If the sun grew too hot, we took sanctuary inside the dormitories and ran wild through the empty lobbies and lounges. Occasionally we broke things, like a vending machine, and would slink away, covering our tracks as best we could. We were always the first in line for lunch, crowding impatiently at the entrance to the cafeteria as the comrades began trickling back from their morning sessions. When we were finally allowed in, we rushed rudely ahead of everyone to load our trays with goodies, going back for seconds and thirds, becoming so stuffed that we had no choice but to leave behind entire plates of uneaten spaghetti and pie.

When lunch was over, the comrades congregated on the lawn to play a few minutes of volleyball before the afternoon meetings began.

"Hey, kids, let's sing a song," said a comrade with a guitar.

And we gathered around on the grass as the man sang, "I'm tired of the boss exploiting me. I'm tired of being oppressed." His voice deep and loud, his fingers moving up and down the guitar.

"I'm tired of the boss exploiting me," we sang along. "I'm tired of being oppressed."

Then the comrade asked us to suggest someone else who

exploited and oppressed us, and as he strummed the notes we all thought long and hard but couldn't come up with anyone.

"Come on, guys, I know you can think of someone."

"Teacher," a girl finally offered, and we all agreed, but the comrade said that was wrong, that the teacher was a worker too and just as exploited as anybody. So no one knew what to say. It was apparent that the comrade was growing frustrated, and finally he said, "Landlord." And so we all sang, "I'm tired of the landlord exploiting me. I'm tired of being oppressed."

One evening, toward the end of the week, my sister came and found me, and together we walked hand in hand to the cafeteria on the other side of campus, where my father ate his meals. Our pace was rapid and focused, and I rushed to tell her about my many adventures from the week.

"Hey, Jamileh," a comrade called out, "is that your little brother? I didn't know you had a little brother."

Along the way we passed a small table covered with pamphlets and surrounded by sad men who had been expelled from the party years ago. "Those are not comrades," my mother had once scolded me when I had gone over to their table to say hi. "They're here to cause problems."

"The revolution needs a revolutionary party," the men said to my sister imploringly, coming toward her with their pamphlets outstretched. "The revolution needs . . ."

But my sister ignored them and put her arm around my shoulder and steered me away.

At dinner I was exceedingly polite. I sat bolt upright in my chair, ate in moderation, and tried not to spill anything. I also made sure to say please and thank you.

"Hey, old man," my brother shouted to my father with a joking familiarity that frightened me, "can you hand over the salt and pepper shakers?"

"Yass, yass," my father said, his long arm reaching from far away.

"Yass, yass," my brother said, imitating his accent.

"Yass, yass," my sister said.

As the meal progressed, the table grew wild with a carnival of voices that contended for my father's attention. There was something kingly about the way he sat there, a friendly king, his hands laying flat on the table as he listened respectfully to the Iranian comrades who had pulled up a chair to discuss the Shah. They spoke in Persian first, and then in English, so that American comrades could also offer their views. And then my brother and sister, who had now affected a cultured, sophisticated air, took out their notebooks and pens and also plunged their way into the conversation.

Amid the rising chaos, my father's girlfriend put her arm around the back of my chair and took the opportunity to teach me things I had already learned a long time ago. "This is a circle," she said with friendship, tracing her finger around the rim of my chocolate-milk glass. Her name was Dianne, and I was aware that she was the opposite of my mother.

She was tall and confident and had once run for senator of California, whereas my mother was short and anxious and worked as a secretary. She was also prettier than my mother and had long hair, and this made me feel troubled. I knew that she was my father's girlfriend, and from my six-year-old way of thinking I thought that this meant that she had become my brother and sister's mother.

Midway through the meal I got the overwhelming urge to tell my father something, to tell him something about my day, but I did not know how to get his attention because I did not know what to call him. In nursery school I had had a teacher who was Filipino and whose name I could not pronounce, so I had taken to prefacing anything I said with "Hey, guess what!" I said it so often that it must have begun to sound like I was saying it as if it were her name—maybe I even began to think that it was her name—because one afternoon a teacher said to me sharply, "Her name is not 'hey, guess what.' "

"Hey, guess what!" I shouted at my father. The table fell silent. My father looked at me from behind his round glasses—round glasses on a round face. His stomach was also round and it pressed against the table. He was bald but had stubble on his face. His skin was dark because he was Iranian.

"I climbed the tree behind the library!" I said.

My father blinked his eyes. "Say, is that so?" he said as if this was special news. "The tree behind the library."

"Like a monkey," I said.

"Like a monkey," he repeated.

The table laughed. My brother and sister looked at me with disappointment.

"He's so cute," one of the women comrades said, and reached over and rubbed my head. And then someone said something about the Shah, and my father's attention was quickly drawn back to the matter at hand.

Dianne picked up a napkin and said to me, "This is a square."

The final night of the convention, everyone convened in the campus chapel for the fund-raiser. I sat next to my mother in the first row of the balcony and looked down over the railing. I knew that somewhere below was the rest of my family, and I also knew that sometime during the week my mother and father had met briefly, courteously, but I had not been privy to that meeting. Now I could see only a great mass of comrades filling the pews and overflowing the aisles, the hum of conversation excited and eager. When everyone had taken their seats, the speakers approached the podium and one after another they laid out in detail the unhappy situation of the world. "Comrades, the ruling class is consolidating power . . ." I could sense a heavy, brooding silence blanketing the audience and I sat as still as possible, feeling the somber mood drape me. "Comrades, we are on the verge of a worldwide depression . . ."

But at some point the speeches began to change in tone

as they described the state of the Socialist Workers Party, and what had been accomplished that week, and what would be accomplished that year, and the various projects the party was undertaking, like modernizing the printing press, for instance, and how much more effective the party would be in fighting the ruling class once this printing press had been modernized and all the *Militant*s and books and pamphlets could be printed more efficiently and cheaply. And now, as the speakers spoke, the audience began to come alive with energy and optimism, and the first tentative bursts of applause broke out, short bursts that soon grew longer and more sustained until it was time for Jack Barnes, national secretary and leader of the party, to take the podium.

"Comrades," he said, and the chapel fell quiet with expectation as he adjusted the microphone and looked out into the sea of faces and then up into the balcony.

I was unnerved by Barnes and I always dreaded his appearance. He was a thin, bald, plain man—from Minneapolis—with a long face and a sharp voice, who would be wholly unremarkable looking were it not for the gruesome fact that he was missing his left arm about two inches below the elbow. He had the unfortunate preference for wearing short-sleeved shirts, and when he gestured, the remaining fragment of his forearm would swivel back and forth, causing me to believe that he was in ghostly possession of a full arm, a full hand, full fingers that were pointing emphatically toward the struggles ahead. It reminded me of a worm that, after being cut in two, continues to live.

"Comrades," he said to the rapt audience. "Comrades, the Socialist Workers Party is now at the vanguard of the working class."

And at that the chapel erupted. Long, loud, and continuous. Everyone clapped and stomped, including my mother. On it went, as if it might go on forever. I am sure my brother and sister and father and Dianne clapped and stomped as well. I joined too, pounding my bare feet on the wooden floor, adding to the tumult. The building shook and vibrated with sound, trembled with it. And finally, after much time had elapsed, Jack Barnes put out his one good arm to calm the audience. "Comrades, please," he said. "Comrades, please. I've just been informed that the applause is threatening to compromise the chapel's structure." Which, of course, made everyone applaud and stomp even louder.

And then it was time to collect the money.

Early the next morning I congregated with Frankie and the other children in the cafeteria and stuffed my face one last time with pancakes and waffles. Then I said good-bye until next year and went to my dorm room and packed my suitcase and put on my shoes and went with my mother to the lobby, which was now being emptied of the banners about the Vietnam War and the Fourth International.

"Let me help with those suitcases," a comrade said, and I

followed them out to the long line of Greyhound buses that sat waiting to be boarded.

On the wide, clean sidewalk, I walked up and down among the luggage, looking for my brother and sister, but eventually I was told that they had already left for Brooklyn and that they had said to tell me they would see me soon, definitely soon. And then my mother and I climbed aboard our bus and the driver pulled away. Through the window I watched as the campus receded into the distance.

Weeks later, months later, after the memories had begun to fade, I would sometimes crawl onto my mother's lap when she returned from her secretarial job, tired and unhappy, and I would sit with her quietly, just the two of us. Her arms would enfold me and she would press me against her and I would feel her breathing, her chest rising and falling.

In the warm stillness I would sometimes ask her when she thought the revolution was going to come.

"When will it come, Ma?"

"Soon," she'd answer, quickly brightening, smiling. "It's inevitable."

"Will I be seven years old?" I'd ask.

"Well, no," she'd say with the greatest of patience. "The revolution is going to take a bit longer than that."

"Will I be ten?"

"No."

"Will I be eleven?"

"No."

"Will I be eighteen?"

And then she'd say, "Yes, Saïd. Yes. You'll be eighteen. When you're eighteen the revolution will come."

5

ONE OF THE BENCHMARKS FOR being a dedicated member of the Socialist Workers Party is the willingness to open your home to comrades who might be traveling to New York City to help out with a campaign, or to give a speech, or to modernize a printing press. Communists should have no sentimental attachment to their homes; they are there to provide shelter, and like any other material object—socks or spoons—they are good only as long as they are useful. "After the revolution comes," my mother would tell me, "people will live wherever they want to live, because private property will be a thing of the past."

And so just a few months before I turned five years old, my mother agreed to let a comrade stay with us for a few days while he was in the city from San Francisco to help renovate the party's national office. We had my brother and sister's spare bedroom, after all.

"I am ——," the comrade said upon his entry into our home, shaking my mother's hand. His face was wide and friendly, covered with a beard and topped with a huge head of hair that made him look something like a lumberjack.

"I'm Martha Harris," my mother said. "It's nice to meet you. Please come in. Set your bags down anywhere. I'll show you around. This is my son Saïd."

The man knelt down in front of me and put out his hand.

"It's nice to meet you, Saïd," he said.

"You look like a lumberjack," I said forthrightly, and this made him shake with laughter.

On the first evening, in order to repay my mother for the kindness she showed in opening her home to him (although such sacrifice was of course made selflessly), he repaired a lamp of ours that had been broken for some time.

I watched him repair it.

"First I'm going to make sure it's unplugged," he said to me patiently. "Now I'm going to take off the lamp shade. Now I'm going to unscrew this screw."

I was even allowed to hand him some of the tools, but my hands were so small that the tools clattered to the floor in the midst of the exchange. My mother and the guest found this adorable.

When the man had finished tinkering, he turned the switch and the room was filled with light.

"Look how wonderful," my mother said.

On the second evening, we all sat down together for dinner. This was unusual, as no man had ever eaten with us before. I was awed by the tremendous amount that the comrade consumed, spoonful after spoonful disappearing into his mouth. The comrade was also extremely gracious, and he would ask for the salt politely, almost daintily, and he would pass the butter if you needed it and he complimented my mother's cooking and he said that I was such a good boy.

On the third evening, the comrade offered to babysit me while my mother attended a meeting.

No. My mother couldn't possibly ask that of the man.

It was no bother for him.

Was he sure?

Sure he was sure.

She'd be home by eleven.

Take your time.

Very nice of you.

And then my mother, happy to be free and unencumbered, kissed me on the head, told me to behave, picked up her knapsack, and closed the door behind her, shutting me inside, alone with a man whom she did not know except insofar as he was a revolutionary—and therefore a friend. A comrade.

"Let's play," the comrade said.

I was ecstatic, and I immediately reinvented the games my brother and I had played in the apartment.

"Look at me! I'm a monster!" I cried out.

"I'm so afraid," the comrade cried, fleeing from me and cowering behind a chair. I was gleeful of such feigned terror.

My mother was blocks away now, descending the steps to the subway, fumbling in her bag for the token, dropping it in the turnstile, pushing through, looking down the empty tracks, wondering how long the train would take.

"The monster is coming to get me!"

My giggles filled the apartment as the subway arrived, as

my mother entered, took a seat, crossed her legs, took out something to read, rocked on the train as it hurtled underground toward Manhattan.

When I had exhausted myself with being the monster, the comrade became the monster and did what my mother could not do, stooping down to pick me up by my legs and swing me over his shoulder. His power thrilled me.

"The monster has caught you! The monster has caught you!"

"The monster has caught me!" Laughing. Laughing.

"You're laughing too much," the comrade said, and his false entreaties made me laugh more.

And then my mother's stop arrived, and she exited the subway and walked outside and around the corner onto Broadway and up the elevator to the eighth floor of the Socialist Workers Party meeting hall, where she greeted everyone.

And now I was sitting on the comrade's lap in my underwear, and his face was larger now, closer now, his hands tickling me under my arms, then beneath my shirt, and then on my calves. And I wondered how I had ended up in my underwear.

"Stop laughing," the comrade teased. "No more laughing."

His voice was near my ear, booming away, and I could feel his hands traveling up toward my knees, then past my knees. I squealed in his grasp.

"If you keep laughing you're going to make yourself sick."

Then his hands were on my thighs, then higher.

And as I squirmed to free myself from his arms, and as

my mother took her seat and waited for the speaker to take the microphone, the comrade pulled the elastic of my underpants back and put his hand inside, sending a shockwave coursing through my body.

"Comrades, thank you all for coming," the first speaker of the night intoned.

"You're sick," the comrade said to me with playful banter. "You've made yourself sick. The doctor is now going to have to perform an important operation."

Then he unzipped his pants.

6

FOR NINE HOURS A DAY, five days a week, I sit in a white, bright office that belongs to Martha Stewart, the billionaire empress of all things homemaking. My job is to assist in the graphic design of boxes and bags and labels and tags, which will ultimately be filled with or pasted onto things like plates and lamps and sheets and burgundy sheer voile curtains. It is a boring job, to be sure, mindless and repetitive and without thanks, but it is a supreme pleasure to immerse myself daily in the lush fantasies of pink and chartreuse, while surrounded by pretty young women and the smell of cake baking in the test kitchen. From time to time, I will catch sight of Martha, tall, blond, majestic—confoundingly the same name as my mother—as she walks briskly through the hallway en route to another meeting that will make her richer than she already is. I have worked for her for several years, but she is utterly unaware of my existence. I am positive, though, that one day she will notice me, smile at me—"Who are you?" she will say—and she will invite me to spend the weekend as a guest in one of her palatial estates in Maine or Connecticut or Westchester, where I will gladly, and without reservation, go.

In the meantime, I have been infected by her sense of style.

Just a couple months ago my coworker Karen gave me some extra pillowcases to take home. Back in my studio apartment I happily exchanged my old gray-white pillow-cases that I'd had for five years for the fresh lavender ones, picturing a girlfriend—Karen?—resting her head on them. Once the pillowcases were installed, though, I noticed how gray-white my sheets were and they, too, had to go. And once the sheets went, the blankets had to go. With each new arrival, no matter how small, I marveled at how transfigured my apartment became. And how transfigured I felt inside of my apartment. So on and so forth my purchases went, until I have reached my latest adventure of standing, staring, in the middle of the aisle at Bed Bath & Beyond trying to choose among an exhaustive array of tissue holders. I had no idea that there were so many styles.

It doesn't matter, though. I've already concluded that brushed metal is by far the most attractive choice, the most sophisticated choice, and it is the one that I want.

"$24.99," the price tag reads.

Which presents me with a quandary, because for $16.99 I can purchase the stainless-steel tissue holder, which is, when I stop to consider, pretty much the same as the brushed metal. And wouldn't it be the sensible thing to save myself eight dollars? Of course, the sensible thing would be not to buy any tissue holder at all, as a tissue holder is a near-meaningless contrivance. When I was a child, my mother didn't own a tissue holder, as the tissue already came in a box and what would be the need to hold something that was already being held? There were times even when we didn't have tissue at all and instead relied on toilet paper to blow our noses. My dilemma, therefore, runs deep.

I feel the distant, nagging impulse to steal. It originates in my shoulders and extends into my hands. It would cleanly resolve the situation. I've stolen frequently throughout my life, from stores, people, and places of employment. Sometimes I was caught and rebuked, but often I got away. The things I took were always things I could afford but would not permit myself to buy. When I was thirteen years old I stole a stack of comic books from a 7-Eleven and was chased five blocks by the cashier. I ran for my life, barely able to breathe, my limbs swinging wildly. As I rounded the corner of my friend's apartment building, I slipped and fell and the comic books went skittering over the pavement. I had no choice but to leave them in order to save myself. Down into my friend's basement I ran, with the cashier on my heels. "Someone please stop him!" He had the comic books, but now he wanted justice. The first door I came to was the laundry room, and when I went inside I realized with horror that I had unwittingly cornered myself. There was no time, however, to turn and leave. In the corner was a blue wooden door, and I hurried and opened it. At first blush it was just a small dark closet, but when I stuck my head inside and looked to the right I saw a toilet bowl. I could hear the cashier coming, so I sat down on the toilet and closed the door behind me. Now that I was at rest, sweat began to drip down my chest and forehead, and the sound of my breathing was loud and labored. At the very last second I noticed a silver latch dangling from the door, but as I reached up to secure it, the footsteps entered the laundry room and I pulled my hand away. I held my breath and waited. There was silence. And then the footsteps approached the door directly. It swung open. Light poured in. All the cashier had to do was stick his head in and look to the right, where he would find the criminal sitting on the toilet, but miraculously he did not think to do this, and the door closed as quickly as it had opened, and the footsteps receded from the laundry room, and after a sufficient amount of time had passed I stood up, brushed myself off, and went upstairs to my friend's apartment. *Any crime against society is a good crime.*

I'm not a thief anymore. I'm too old and I've come too far. The impulse remains, though. It will be there forever, I'm sure. All around me in Bed Bath & Beyond customers, young and old, fill their baskets and shopping carts with all sorts of items. They find their many options delightful. And all at once, like a magnet leaping from the refrigerator of its own accord, I grasp the brushed-metal tissue holder in my hand and walk briskly, purposefully, toward the cashier. *$24.99.* The metal gleams. How nice it will look in my bathroom. I will light a candle and I will take a bath and I will look at my tissue holder. That is what I will do tonight.

And then I will come back next week and buy a shower curtain.

7

ON A FRIGID AFTERNOON ONE January, just after my seventh birthday, I stood alone in a strange neighborhood, unable to unlock a door.

"Pay attention, Saïd," my mother had told me the day before while she had demonstrated how to use the key. There was apparently an imperfection somewhere in the key's relationship to the lock, but if it was jiggled just so and at just the right angle, the door would pop open. It had looked easy enough when my mother had done it, yet as I stood there the following day by myself, trying to turn the key first one way and then the other, and then fitting it in upside down, and then trying to force it with brute strength—which was an act of desperation—the lock could not be unlocked. Was it the wrong door?

It was getting dark and I knew my mother would not be home for several hours. To further complicate matters, I was not dressed properly for the cold. My coat was more of a jacket than a coat, and I had no hat or hood. The mittens I wore were not conducive to such a delicate operation as unlocking a door, but when I took them off, my hands froze and the key fell to the ground. The door had been equipped with a storm door, and as I worked at the lock, the wind from the river blew, causing this extra door to flutter and bang against me. I also had to go to the bathroom.

Sitting nearby was a discarded refrigerator with its door still intact. "That's dangerous," my mother had told me in the middle of our lesson. "You could suffocate inside it." Together we had tried to turn it around so that the door would face the wall and be inaccessible, but my mother was a small woman, and I was a small child, and the two of us had not been strong enough. "The landlord should be doing this," my mother had said to me, at me, as if I might be the landlord, "but I'm sure the bastard doesn't give a damn!"

A black woman about my mother's age had passed by with her son, who was also about my age, and my mother had called out to her abruptly, "Say! Do you live around here? Say! Excuse me! Do you live around here?"

The woman had blinked back, confused. "What did you say to me?" It must have been an unusual question to have been posed so unexpectedly by a stranger—a white stranger—and the woman seemed to take it as an affront.

"This refrigerator," my mother said, pointing at it as if it were alive, "the landlord won't take it away. Make sure you don't let your son play around it."

The woman had nodded and said okay, but still she seemed unable to discern by my mother's tone if she was being helpful or hostile. Then she took her boy by the hand and the two of them walked off.

Our flight from Brooklyn had felt clandestine: things thrust in boxes hastily, like we were planning an escape. Furniture was sold for whatever the buyer was willing to pay. I watched it all go. With the help of a dozen comrades, my mother had loaded the moving van on a cold, sunny afternoon in December, four days before my seventh birthday. Able to carry only the lightest things, I had watched like a spectator as the boxes were placed one on top of the other, balancing high, all the unsold things of our life, even a potted plant. When it was time for us to embark, Britton emerged from our apartment building and put out his hand like an adult. Where had he learned how to make such a gesture? "Good-bye," he said. I shook his hand. "Good-bye."

By choosing Pittsburgh, my mother was again following the bread crumbs that led to her brother Mark, who was now an English professor at the University of Pittsburgh, basking in the acclaim of his motion picture *Bang the Drum Slowly. A film everybody will cheer!* the advertisements said. It was my uncle who had been the one to suggest that a single mother with a child would have an easier life in a slower, smaller city like Pittsburgh. And it was only because of him and his largesse that, in the beginning, life for me seemed fanciful and the exact opposite of hardship. For the first week my mother and I lived with him and his family in his enormous house, which had a piano, soft carpeting, a backyard, a light-blue Mercedes, a black maid, and an extraordinary painting, twenty feet wide, maybe thirty, of a partially unwrapped chocolate bar. When I passed this chocolate bar hanging in the landing of the staircase, I wanted to stick my hand right into it and grab a piece and stuff it into my mouth and face the consequences of my action. My uncle was pleasant and

friendly, a head and nose full of white hair, and would surface now and then from his den to speak to me as if I were
an adult: "Martha tells me that you also have an interest in
literature." I spent most of my days playing with my cousin
Henry, who was six years older and had built an elaborate toy
village in his basement, with miniature houses and cars and
people and through which wound an electric train. I would
watch endlessly, tirelessly, as he steered the locomotive round
and round.

I assumed, of course, that this was my home now and that
I would live in it with them forever. But for some reason, only
a week after my mother and I had arrived, we packed our
suitcases and went elsewhere. The next house we found was
not a house but a one-bedroom apartment that belonged to a
cheerful couple from the Socialist Workers Party named Ed
and Carla, who had graciously allowed us to stay with them.
At night, since there was no extra bed or couch, my mother
and I would cover ourselves with a blanket and fall asleep side
by side on the living-room floor. In the morning, after Ed
and Carla had left for their factory jobs, I would wash myself
in the sink, since the bathtub had not been equipped with a
faucet. After that, my mother would leave me behind in the
strange home while she undertook the daunting, insurmountable tasks of finding a job, an apartment, and an elementary
school, the latter search made even more arduous by the fact
that we had arrived in the middle of a teachers' strike.

For my seventh birthday my uncle had given me one
of those plastic View-Master toys that you look into like
binoculars while clicking through three-dimensional images

that tell a variety of stories like Cinderella or Snow White. I had been given only one story with the gift—Superman—and during the day I would sit alone in the silent, unfamiliar apartment and stare over and over through the thing, clicking past the same dozen pictures of Superman flying high above the skyline en route to rescuing someone. I kept thinking that the story would somehow change to something new, or that I would see something in it that I hadn't seen before, but it remained as it always was. Eventually I grew so ill of it, almost on the verge of real illness, that I resorted to a math workbook that had also been given to me as a gift. It turned out to be slightly beneath my aptitude, and so I was able to pass the hours by compulsively penciling in answers to problems that were without challenge. In the evening, when my mother returned from scouring the unknown city, she would sit next to me on the living-room floor and carefully check my work one by one, all of it without error. Then we would cover ourselves with the blanket and fall asleep.

The home my mother finally found for us was a one-bedroom apartment on the ground floor of a small brick building in the middle of a ghetto. To get to it our first night, my mother and I boarded a bus filled with exhausted passengers, most of them black. We carried with us several bags of clothes and a broom. I had never known anyone to be on a bus with a broom, and I felt embarrassed to be seen with it and began to have a keen sense that something had gone far off-kilter. We rode for a while through dark Pittsburgh streets, until my mother was certain we had missed our stop and had to ask a fellow passenger if the bus was going in the right direction. The passenger did not know the answer, nor did the next passenger, nor did the bus driver, until it became clear to everyone involved that my mother was stressing the wrong syllable of the name of the street so that it was rendered incomprehensible to native Pittsburghers. Eventually we passed a Howard Johnson's restaurant, and a gas station, and a parking lot, and shortly after that it was time for us to get off.

Through the neighborhood we walked, with the bags and the broom. It was very dark out, and I imagined that the lighted windows in the houses were eyes observing us as we passed. Halfway to our new home, my mother realized that it was past dinnertime and we had not yet eaten and had no groceries, so we turned and went back the way we had come, the eyes watching us return, and walked to the Howard Johnson's. Sitting beside the bags and the broom—I had never known anyone to sit in a restaurant with a broom—I ate a hot dog and a pickle. For dessert my mother ordered for me, as a special treat, an ice cream sundae in the shape of a snowman dressed in a candy suit with a smiling chocolate face. It was disconcerting to be given such a thing, it was not at all consistent with my mother's character, and I knew in that moment, and without equivocation, that something was terribly wrong with us.

"Look at the funny ice cream man," my mother said, but it was the voice of a performer.

The snowman grinned up at me wildly. I felt indebted.

"Look how funny!" my mother said from the stage.

I picked up my spoon and gobbled him down.

Despite being occupied by other tenants, our new apartment building radiated a feeling of having been abandoned years earlier, decades earlier, neglected and unrepaired. The floors of the apartment were uneven and slanted toward the middle, causing the furniture to lean forward precariously away from the walls, as if it were preparing to take flight. The carpeting was brown, or green, or had once been green, but had been worn down and away by the feet of previous generations. If you stepped too heavily in the kitchen, the living room vibrated; if you tried to shut the bedroom door, it wouldn't close completely; if you took a bath, the tub wouldn't drain. The place, no matter how much you scrubbed, could not be cleaned. There were only a few small windows, and if it was a sunny day, the sunlight could not penetrate. Pittsburgh climate being what it is, most days were without sun, and so the rooms grew dark long before it was night. The front door of our apartment opened directly out onto the sidewalk, giving the distressing perception that anyone passing by on the street could walk into our home unannounced. In my bed at night, I would watch the headlights from passing cars illuminate the bedroom with red and yellow streaks of light, thinking that one wrong move and the car would come crashing through.

If the neighborhood had ever amounted to anything, it

was a long time ago. Now the only claim it could make was the fading memory that forty years earlier Andy Warhol had lived there as a little boy. The street I lived on was called Ophelia Street, and it was narrow and fronted on either side by worn-out brick houses packed tightly together and inhabited by ex-steelworkers. There was a playground nearby with swings and a giant metal turtle that could be climbed on top of, or under, but no children were ever seen. Across the street from our apartment was a small corner store that sold candy and soda and did a brisk business, but other than that the area had a deserted feel, a ghost town where only a few remaining holdouts continued to live. One block away was the Monongahela River. In a few miles it would connect with the Allegheny, and the two together would form the Ohio. For more than a century these three rivers had been busy day and night, bringing in coal and taking out steel, but by the time my mother and I arrived, the steel industry was collapsing, and one century of booming prosperity was coming to an end, leaving Pittsburgh an aged and decimated city. The Monongahela River carried nothing now, lying empty and still like a parking lot that had been thoughtlessly constructed in the middle of nowhere. Our neighborhood sloped down toward the water and gave the impression that in due time all the streets and houses would slide completely into it and be no longer.

Up the hill from us, strategically placed so as to be easily accessible to the downtrodden of the neighborhood, was the headquarters for the Pittsburgh branch of the Socialist Workers Party, both meeting hall and bookstore, with twenty or so members. It was a small building, just a few rooms and a basement, with a storefront that was always pasted with signs calling out to the workers.

Our move to this neighborhood and to this apartment made me feel that I had descended from a great height and fallen hard to earth. For this reason I took to referring to our apartment as "the cave," and my mother, rather than seeing this as a troubling indicator, instead found it delightful, asking me to repeat it to comrades, who also found it delightful.

"Go on, Saïd, tell Ed and Carla and Bill and Ginny what you said about our new apartment. . . ." And I would repeat it, finding myself strangely happy, reveling in the gales of laughter that greeted me.

The difference between us and the other poor families in this neighborhood was that our poverty was intentional and self-inflicted. A choice chased after, as opposed to a reality that could not be avoided. There was no compelling reason for such deprivation. From the secondhand clothing to the secondhand furniture, from the unpaid library books to the unbought skateboard, it was all artifice. We were without money, yes, but we were not without options. My mother was highly literate, well read, well spoken, and she held an undergraduate degree in English literature from a time when many women did not even attend college. Not to mention that fif-

teen minutes away lived a wealthy brother who had generously helped her throughout the years, had even helped pay
her tuition when she had wanted to return to school. Then
there was the matter of the missing husband, who, with some
cajoling—or the cajoling of the judicial system—could be
pressed into aiding us.

Instead, my mother actively, consciously, chose not only
for us to *be* poor but for us to *remain* poor, and the two
of us suffered greatly for it. Because to suffer and to suffer
greatly was the point. It was the fulfillment of ourselves. My
mother was no doubt emboldened by the philosophy that
there was honor in wretchedness, virtue in misery, nobility
in hardship. Members of the Socialist Workers Party might
outwardly deride Christian ideals extolling poverty and the
renunciation of material goods, but inwardly they were convinced that there was nothing more ignominious than to
succeed in a society that was as morally bankrupt as ours.
It was no accident that almost every comrade was from a
middle-class background and had repudiated their upbring-
ing and their college degrees in order to pursue a higher, more
profound calling. If you flourished in this society, you flourished because you were deviant and unethical, an exploiter
of the working class. Marx had believed that it was the oppressed who would inherit the earth, and every communist
since him had believed it as well, including Lenin, Trotsky,
and the members of the Socialist Workers Party. My mother
and I lived within a slightly retailored version of the Sermon
on the Mount—but only slightly. When the revolution

finally arrived, we would stand first among the deserving. My mother would see to it.

I was not without my own resources in this neighborhood. I refused to be without them. A week or so after our arrival, I was befriended by a boy a year or two older than I, blond-haired and blue-eyed, named Michael March. He was also the single child of a single mother, and he was also left to his own devices, but while my early life had caused me to shield myself from danger and confrontation and turn inward, his had caused him to seek out precarious situations and place himself in the middle of them. "I don't think it's a good idea to play with that boy," my mother had said upon meeting him, sensing danger—and she had been right. Not more than ten years later he'd kill himself playing Russian roulette with a group of friends.

One night, as we wandered the neighborhood looking for something to do, I had unwittingly followed him up the stairs to the front door of a stranger's house. Hardly registering what was transpiring before me, I watched as he soundlessly turned the doorknob and crawled into the home unannounced. Unable to turn away—because I had nowhere else to go—I had slunk after him down the dim hallway. From an adjacent room came the sounds of the family at dinner. It was a peculiar, distressing sensation to be inside a stranger's home when the stranger did not know I was there. The house felt haunted and I knew, distantly, that I was the one doing the haunting. Silently, Michael and I had crawled on our hands and knees down into the basement, where, in the clammy darkness, we rummaged through boxes of old clothes and books until we found what it was we were after: toys. Through the box we went, examining each ball and game and car, as if we had been taken on a shopping spree. Finally I settled on a Barbie doll in a pink dress, one shoe missing. Michael, in response, took for himself Barbie's boyfriend, Ken. That we had allowed ourselves only one toy apiece was a bizarre limit in what could have been a limitless transgression. Just as the two of us were preparing to make our getaway, we heard the family's conversation cease abruptly, and the sound of a chair scraping out from the table, and vigorous male footsteps rapidly approaching overhead. In a panic, we scurried around the basement looking for a place to save ourselves. Michael managed to conceal himself expertly beneath the laundry table. "Hide me!" I had whispered in desperation, but there was room for only one. Not knowing what to do, I had buried my head in my hands in the hope that if I could not see, I could not be seen. But the footsteps passed over and faded away, and once we were sure the family had safely resumed their dinner, the two of us crawled back the way we had come, our hands and knees making impressions in the carpeting. Later that night, in Michael's empty apartment, showing no signs of remorse, we stripped Barbie and Ken of their clothes and, in feverish child's play, pressed their plastic bodies against each other.

Not very long after that, with my mother still unemployed and the teachers still on strike, she and I woke one day before dawn and, along with a few other comrades, caught a Greyhound bus to Richmond, Virginia. The ride took six hours, and the combination of the cold winter air, the stale heat blowing through the vents, the uncomfortable seats, and the incessant swerving along highways caused me, midway through the trip, to vomit into an empty paper cup that my mother held in front of my mouth. It felt like an act of penance for what I had done with Michael, and I accepted it as such. Once in Richmond, we had joined about five hundred other protesters, mostly women, including comrades from other branches, and listened to speaker after speaker, also mostly women, as they demanded that Virginia pass the Equal Rights Amendment.

Richmond was no warmer than Pittsburgh, but I accepted this also as penance. When the last speaker had spoken, all five hundred of us marched through downtown toward the statehouse, chanting and holding our banners aloft, passing shoppers and office workers who stopped to stare at us curiously as if we were a circus come to town. I felt the familiar sensation of being naked, on display, a monkey being led through the streets for the townspeople to gape at. A woman leading the throng chanted through her bullhorn, "Hey, hey, what do you say? Ratify the ERA!" Voices rose up in unison, and soon my mother joined the chorus, her voice sounding frail in the open air of the city. I shouted along as well. To remain silent would have made me conspicuous in the eyes of both the bystanders and the people with whom I was marching.

"What do we want?" the bullhorn asked.

"The ERA!" I screamed.

"When do we want it?"

"Now!" I screamed.

There was comfort in being able to see the problem before me, contained and defined, and understanding clearly what the remedy for that problem was. There was comfort also in knowing that there were five hundred other people who understood this problem as well. And as I marched and shouted, I began to feel that we were the ones who were on the inside and those who stood idly on the sidewalks with their bags and their briefcases were on the outside, lost and confused. They were the circus, and *I* had come to watch *them*.

When we finally arrived at the Virginia statehouse, a few women took the microphone to again make our demands known. Behind them was a well-scrubbed flight of stairs ascending toward a gigantic white building surrounded by impassive columns. "The seat of ruling-class power," my mother had said with bitterness. Its grand, imperial architecture had a sobering effect on the day's events, putting into perspective what the odds really were. By late afternoon the protest broke up, and with the winter sun beginning to set, my mother and I rode six hours back to Ophelia Street on the Greyhound bus, where I once again, midway through, vomited into an empty paper cup that my mother held before my mouth.

After that, my mother landed a job as a secretary at Carnegie Mellon University, and the teachers' strike ended, and I found myself standing in front of a door that I could not open. Was it the wrong door?

I had worked at the lock calmly at first, operating under the premise that it would only be a matter of time before it would click. I had assumed that the defect was in me, not the lock, but soon I began to feel that I was attempting something that could never be achieved. It was freezing, and I sensed that I was in grave danger, or would soon be. I thought perhaps I should go to Michael's house, but I was so unfamiliar with the neighborhood that I didn't know how to get there. As the sky darkened toward evening and it grew colder, I became delirious with the thought that eventually the key would find the right groove and the door would swing wide. The key fitting, the door swinging, the key fitting . . . I knocked on the door. "Ma!" I called out, and the sound of my voice startled me, emphasizing the silence of the neighborhood. Then I kicked on the door. I pulled on its knob. Then I pushed on its knob. I knocked again, this time louder and with both fists. "Ma! Ma!" And from down the street I could hear, "Saïd! Saïd!" But when I turned to greet my mother, she was not there.

Without bothering to consider what I was doing, I turned and stood flat against the unyielding door, my back pressing into the cold steel, giving myself up to its mercy. Then I pulled the fluttering storm door closed around me, so that I was sandwiched between the two doors, protected as best I could against the elements. My head reached just high enough that I was able to look through the glass of the storm door, out onto the world. There was nothing to observe. Everything was blank. It grew darker. It grew colder. The wind picked up. The storm door rattled. In the darkness the refrigerator smiled at me, its white body glowing like it was alive and well. I imagined my mother arriving at any moment, now, now, now. Then I imagined Michael March coming to find me. After that, I imagined my uncle's light-blue Mercedes rounding the corner.

At one point, two older boys came running down the street, happily tossing a football back and forth. They stopped for a minute in front of my building, laughing loudly and chasing the football as it bounced around and beneath parked cars. Their shouts flew in the face of the general order of things, as if they were violating a code of conduct of the neighborhood. Then they decided to take a shortcut through a small opening beside my building, and as they did they noticed me. I looked at them through the glass and they looked back at me. They hesitated for a moment before walking off, unsettled by the sensation of a door seemingly come to life. Then a small man appeared at the far end of the street and the boys ran on.

I watched the man as he approached. He was wrapped in scarves and bent against the wind, carrying with some difficulty a small bag of groceries that made him look a bit like a cripple, the weight pulling one shoulder unevenly toward the ground. As the man drew closer, the wind blew straight into him and he turned slightly to one side, trying to deflect the blow from his face. Then the wind subsided and the man moved forward quickly until he was directly in front of my door, peering at me through the glass.

"What are you doing in there?" my mother asked, and it was asked with displeasure, as if I was playing a naughty game she had asked me not to play.

"The lock doesn't work, Ma!" I said.

"What do you mean the lock doesn't work?" Again the tone of displeasure, impatience. "It worked this morning. How could it not work now?"

"The key doesn't work, Ma!"

"Which is it?" she said.

"I have to go to the bathroom, Ma!"

She undid the latch of the storm door, and I was released back out into the air of the neighborhood. I handed her the useless key.

"Why didn't you walk over to the party headquarters?" she asked. "It's only a few blocks away." When she said it, I saw myself from above, a bird's-eye view, wandering through foreign streets that crisscrossed one another. "There will always be a comrade there," she said.

The word *comrade* was fluffy and sweet, like cotton candy, and I faulted myself for not having thought of it. The error had been mine.

"Next time," my mother said more gently now.

"Next time," I said.

Then my mother put the disobedient key into the lock, jiggled it once, and the door clicked and swung open as if it had been waiting to do that all along. And the two of us entered our new home, with the boxes still unpacked and the broom propped against the wall.

8

THAT SPRING WE HAD A picnic. All the comrades were there, twenty maybe. Plus about ten "sympathizers," those who were not yet officially comrades but whom everyone hoped would soon decide to be. "They don't have parks like this in New York City," my mother told me. I helped Ed carry cans of soda from the trunk of his car. Ed, whose apartment floor I had slept on not too long ago. I liked Ed. Maybe I even loved him. His hands were big and his arms were strong. Machinist's arms, or steelworker's, or coal miner's. Whatever it was my mother had told me. Today he was shirtless, and his broad chest glistened with sweat. On one of his shoulders was a giant scar—really, many scars, all in a bunch like shredded cheese. He had explained to me that when he was in the military he had gotten a tattoo of an American flag on that shoulder. Then he discovered socialism and had the tattoo destroyed.

Sitting in the shade beneath a tree, my mother spoke animatedly. I watched her hands move up and down in quick succession. "That's right, Martha," a sympathizer said. "You got that right." Some other comrades came and sat down on the grass beside her. Everyone was expecting the arrival soon of an old party veteran who was coming from New York City to give a special speech that weekend. He was due any minute. In the meantime, the grill was started.

I had been to a picnic once before. That was when I lived

in Brooklyn. My brother and sister were there too. I hadn't seen them for a long time. There had been a pond with lily pads, which I played on the edge of all afternoon. At some point I went looking for my brother and sister but was unable to find them among the dozens of comrades. Around and around the pond I went, until it was dark and time to go home. Only at the very last minute did I see them standing together under a tree.

"Where have you been?" I stomped my feet.

They looked at me with startled eyes. "We've been here the whole time."

When the party veteran arrived, we tramped up the hill to greet him at his car. He was bald and wore thick eyeglasses and carried a cane. I was alarmed by how old he was. There were not many old people in the party. Most of them had been driven out over the years by the various factional disputes concerning policy or strategy. *The Shachtmanites. The Cochranites. The Global Class War Faction.* Each time the party had grown smaller, and each time the members had assured themselves that now only those with the correct ideas remained. Somehow, though, this party veteran had managed to endure. Comrades welcomed him warmly and helped him to the picnic table. A paper plate of food was handed to him. He ate slowly. We all sat around and talked about things I did not understand. I drank a can of soda. And then another one. Then I had to pee.

"Don't drink too much," my mother said.

"That's right," Bill said with false admonishment. "No more beer for you." I looked up into his face and grinned. I liked him almost as much as Ed. He also had big hands and strong arms. He also was a machinist or a steelworker. Or he wanted to be. I liked all those who now sat at the picnic table or hovered around the grill. Most of them had come from other branches in other cities. Most of them would one day leave for other branches in other cities. That was the cycle. Tom was a student. And Ginny was about to get a job in a steel mill even though she was a woman. And Mark was going to run for governor so he could "put forward a working-class alternative." And Carla, the woman who lived with Ed, was looking for work in a factory and was good at giving speeches. "Is that his wife?" I had asked my mother. "That's his *companion*," she had corrected. There were no husbands or wives in the party. There were no boyfriends or girlfriends. There were only companions.

As a little boy I assumed that the preponderance of manual laborers in the Socialist Workers Party was the natural result of its appeal among the working class. It was only logical, inevitable, that socialist workers would gravitate to a party of socialist workers. The truth, however, was that the occupations were a contrivance. Most comrades, including my mother, were middle-class students and professionals who had *chosen* to give up their careers for an opportunity at an authentic working-class experience. Experience that would be useful later when the time came to lead the revolution. In 1978 the voluntary nature of this suddenly changed when Jack Barnes, perhaps fearing that the party was still not working class enough, issued an ultimatum that now *required* all members who had not already done so to immediately find work in the industrial sector.

"Every comrade," Barnes wrote, "without exception—employed and unemployed, new and experienced—should now sit down with the leadership and collectively review their situation—their job, their assignment, the city they live in, their various contributions—and decide how they fit into this decision."

Within the party it came to be known as "the turn to industry," or simply "the turn," and it was perceived as a defining moment in the evolution of the party. The immediate result, however, was not revolutionary upsurge but bloodletting of its membership. Many of the doctors, lawyers, and students who had preferred to remain doctors, lawyers, and students simply resigned. And those who did give up their careers and were relocated for industrial work could take cold comfort in the fact that they were now true worker-Bolsheviks in the mold of those worker-Bolsheviks who had fought in the Russian Revolution sixty years earlier. In a report delivered about a year after the initial decree, Barnes admitted to the inherent difficulty in what was being asked. "The turn means a change in the life of thousands and thousands of comrades. . . . Everywhere that we've begun to carry out the turn in a systematic and thorough way, there have been some losses of individual comrades. There are comrades for whom the turn sharply poses the question of what they are doing with their lives, what their personal commitments and priorities are."

Barnes reassures members that, "Comrades cannot be ordered or shamed to make the turn." Just as he reassures them in a subsequent report that, "Of course, there are certain physical and health problems that preclude working in most factories. We know that."

He goes on, though:

> But what we're finding out to our surprise is that many comrades who we might have ruled out six months ago for reasons of health or age, can and are getting into industry. They're politically convinced and inspired. They want to do it. And they get hired. I personally know of a number of comrades in their forties, comrades who have a back problem, or who have had serious operations—they are getting in and finding that they can do it.

It is at this point in the story that Jack Barnes's missing left arm moves from character description to plot point. The portrait that unfolds is of a handicapped man who knows full well he has little chance of being hired even to mop a factory floor, exhorting his membership to abandon all for the glory of industrial life.

My father, the mathematics professor, also managed to dodge the requirement of manual labor. "If I could do it all over again," he has promised me on more than one occasion,

"I would be a factory worker, but unfortunately it's too late for me now. . . ." The statement is always succeeded by a pause that I assume is my cue to reflect on the fact that I, a young man, sit on a cushiony chair in an air-conditioned office owned by a tall blonde named Martha Stewart. My father is a living example of what everyone else in the party could have been: a middle-class, white-collar comrade with summers off. That he has managed to remain such a beloved member is a testament to either his charm or the party's hypocrisy, or a little of both. It doesn't matter, though. The idea that he would ever take a job that demanded he stoop and sweat is absurd. That is not why my father became a member of the party. Lenin's famous maxim, "Every cook has to learn how to govern the state," does not work in reverse and suggest that Lenin was desirous of being a cook.

My brother and sister, however, spent their youth working their way through sweatshops and auto plants and cookie factories. I have a box full of letters with postmarks from places like Winston-Salem, Harrisburg, San Jose, Detroit, as they were continually on the move to the city with the industry that the party had come to believe was now the essential industry for galvanizing the working class. There was something exciting and heroic to me about my brother's and sister's adventures with machines and tools. Each time I saw them at Oberlin or in their rare visits to Pittsburgh, they would look like they had been transformed yet again, older, stronger, more worldly. I would ask them to tell me stories of where they had worked. And they would laughingly describe the factories and the bosses and the assembly lines they toiled on upward of twelve hours a day, fitting this small piece into that other small piece, over and over again until their brains went numb.

My mother, the secretary, did not participate in the party's turn to industry: She was a secretary before and a secretary after. It is the only instance I know of where she resisted what was expected of her. As a young woman she had traded in her dream of being a novelist for what she believed was the more significant work in life, but now, nearly forty-five years old at the time of "the turn," she was not willing to sacrifice again. And while her job as secretary in the fine arts department of Carnegie Mellon University was certainly thankless and unchallenging, there was still something of substance to be gained by being in such close proximity to all those young musicians, actors, singers, painters. Her affection for and attraction to the arts had never been fully extinguished. Nor had her desire to be a writer, and every now and again she would sign up for a writing class—free of charge for university employees—and write a short story. In bed at night I would hear her typing away at the kitchen table, followed by lulls of silent rumination. The stories, which she would ask me to read for her, were almost always about a single mother and her son facing adversity and were written in a tone of unprecedented optimism where the hardships they endured were not so terrible after all.

On days when there were no pressing political demands, she would go to plays, or museums, or movies, sometimes taking me along with her. Together we would sit in the theater as if on a date, watching movies that were far too advanced for me. *Vertigo. Annie Hall. Casablanca*. I was often bored, sometimes frightened, occasionally entertained. She loved books, of course, and she read constantly and then was filled with guilt because of it. "I don't have time to be reading this now," she'd say, but she'd read it anyway, letting her *Militant*s and pamphlets and Pathfinder books wait until tomorrow. If I ever asked what a word meant, she would carry our enormous dictionary to the kitchen table with both hands and page through it, peering, peering, getting sidetracked by other interesting words along the way. "Here it is," she'd finally say. "Look how fascinating it is!" And she would encourage me in the arts as well, enrolling me in music or drawing classes. When I was eight years old, the theater department at Carnegie Mellon cast me in *The Beaver Coat* by Gerhart Hauptmann. Onstage in the blinding lights, I was able to pretend with adults that I was a boy named Philipp, the doctor's son, who had come to pay Mrs. Wolff a visit. "I've been to the zoo and I saw storks!" was my line, which the director told me to shout so that those in the back of the theater could hear.

Now and then on a snow day or in the summertime, my mother would take me with her to her office. At the empty desk beside her, I would play with staplers and paper clips while she typed letters, opened envelopes, answered phones. "Hello, Fine Arts, Dean's Office," I would hear her say over and over again, maybe one hundred times, sometimes even saying it in reflexive error when answering the phone at home. It made me ashamed to see my mother having to work like this. I knew that she was bitter and frustrated.

Her boss, the dean, was a large, soft-bellied Syrian man with gigantic eyeglasses, who seemed friendly enough but of whom I was wary. My mother had me fully aware that we were at the mercy of this man and that our tenuous, unhappy economic life could instantly be made worse by him. "I think he's going to fire me soon," she would tell me on bad days. It was because of him, though, that the theater department had paid me seventy-five dollars for my performance as Philipp, a sum so immense that I was sure I was destined to be a rich and famous actor. When he entered from his adjacent office, I would become as well behaved as possible, hoping that he would send more good fortune our way.

"Saïd," he would say in his accented English, "what will your next role be? Hamlet?"

"I hope so."

And he would laugh, and my mother would laugh, and then he would hand my mother a piece of paper and ask her to type it up.

In the corner of the office sat a grandfather clock with moon and sun faces. The clock chimed every fifteen minutes, with a special chime on the hour, and as I sat at the table and played with the office supplies, I would listen to my mother typing and answering the phone and then the chime as the passage of the day was slowly being marked off. This is the way the years passed. Five years, ten years, fifteen years. My mother would end up keeping the job for thirty years.

When the clock finally struck five, it meant that it was time to go home. And my mother and I would gather our coats and books and whatever uneaten lunch we had stored in the little refrigerator. The dean would call good-bye to me. Outside, the college students could be seen on their way to class or coming back from class, joking, laughing. My mother would take my hand in hers and lead me to the bus stop, where we would wait. Her face a study in exhaustion. Exhaustion from a day of nothingness.

No, there was no need for my mother to make "the turn." She had done it years ago.

9

I WAS A COLLECTOR OF teddy bears. "A connoisseur," my mother said, then she helped me look the word up. At one point I think I had seven of them. Maybe eight. I called them teddy bears, but some were other animals too. "Do you think your stuffed animals are offended that you refer to them all as 'bears'?" my mother would ask. "Maybe," I'd say. I had an opossum, for instance, with a beanbag belly, and also an orange elephant called George that my mother had made for me one Sunday afternoon on her sewing machine while I sat beside her. When she was done, she showed me how to push white stuffing through a small opening she had left in its back. Each night I would get into bed with all of my teddy bears next to me. And in the morning I would wake to find them on the floor or wedged against the wall, imagining that they had gone off on exciting adventures while I slept. Before leaving for school I was always sure to retrieve every one of them, line them up in my bed according to their age, and tuck them in.

My bedroom was as neat as my bed, everything organized and straightened. I made sure never to let it get out of hand. The rest of the apartment, though, felt chaotic and cluttered. Clothes draped chairs, shoes clustered in corners, pencils and pens lay scattered on the floor like leaves in a yard. Furniture was generally positioned haphazardly, aimlessly, without much consideration for the shape of the apartment, as if it had been lugged up two flights to an attic, dropped, and then forgotten. A desk cut off access to the window, a chair sat awkwardly in the middle of the living room. If later my mother was inspired to move my dresser from this side of the bedroom to that side, we were confronted with the additional obstacle of being too weak to do it ourselves and would have to wait patiently until the next time Ed or another male comrade paid us a visit. It was not uncommon for us to eat our meals among the contents of my mother's knapsack, strewn across the table as if spilled in haste.

Add to all of this disarray the many *Militant*s that continued to be amassed week after week, relentless accumulation. My mother saved every single one. To what end I do not know. Never in all my years did I see her referring to them. Their accumulation was quick and significant: forty-eight issues a year. When we moved from Brooklyn to Pittsburgh, when we moved from Ophelia Street to our next apartment, when we moved from that apartment to the next, and the next after that, and after that—half a dozen apartments in two years—they moved with us, each time larger, heavier, more cumbersome, the years all thrown out of order as they were carried to and from the truck by those comrades who had so graciously volunteered to help us move yet again. "One day I should organize all of those," my mother would say, but she never did.

The day after our arrival in the apartment that I would live in long enough to celebrate my eighth birthday, a friendly neighbor knocked on our door to welcome us to the neighborhood. Our new home was a gloomy one-bedroom, just slightly less gloomy than the apartments preceding it and whose best attribute was a deteriorating wooden balcony that hovered precariously over the backyard. The neighbor's arrival gave the unfamiliar surroundings an optimistic air.

"Welcome to the neighborhood," the neighbor said. She was young and pretty and had long dark hair, and she had brought with her, as a housewarming gift, a bottle of grape soda and a half dozen doughnuts. I was instantly charmed.

"Come in," my mother said.

And the young woman stepped inside and stood among the unpacked bags and boxes, the lamps without their lamp shades, and the stacks and stacks of *Militant*s piled dangerously high. I watched from my bedroom doorway as my mother and the neighbor chatted. It was a brief, friendly chat that centered mostly on the nearest supermarket and bus stop. When they were done, my mother thanked her for her time and helpfulness. Just as the young woman was leaving, she casually pointed to the *Militant*s and asked curiously, in an offhand manner, "What are those?" It was an honest question, asked without agenda, but it sounded as if it was colored with unease and perhaps even fright, as if the woman had recoiled and exclaimed, "What are those?!"

My mother heard the question in much the same way as I, but she took pleasure in it, seeing affirmation in revulsion. Later at the party headquarters she repeated the question to everyone, stressing the words so the subtext was made apparent: *"What* are *those?"* The comrades were delighted by the story, affirmed as well, and when my mother had finished relating it, everyone laughed uproariously, including my mother and including me. *"What* are *those?"*

"Stop back sometime," my mother had responded to the young woman, "and we can discuss them." But the young woman never did stop back. And when I had finished the grape soda and the doughnuts, the treats were gone for good. And within a year we had gone to court with the landlord and we were gone for good as well.

10

I HARBOR FANTASTICAL DREAMS OF becoming a famous actor. Dreams born when I yelled twenty-five years earlier about
going to the zoo and seeing storks. This is why I dropped out
of college, why I moved back to New York City, why I never
try for any sort of promotion at work because I've convinced
myself that any additional responsibility will interfere with my
true aspiration. With the notable exception of having been on
the soap opera *Another World* for six episodes, I've had almost
no success. There's a certain amount of awareness deep down
inside me that I'm not very talented. I do my best to ignore
this. Any day now I expect to be discovered by a big film director in much the same way that any day I expect to be discovered by Martha Stewart. And when I do I will use the money
to buy a brownstone in the West Village, where I will live for
the rest of my life feigning weariness of fame and wealth.

This afternoon I need to take an extra-long lunch to go
for an audition. I'm supposed to be working on an urgent set
of labels for a collection of patio furniture, but it'll have to
wait until later.

"Hey, Saïd," Karen calls just as I'm about to walk out the
door.

"I have to run," I say in a panic. "I promise I'll have them
finished by the end of the day."

"I just wanted to tell you," she says, "there's a blueberry pie in the conference room." Karen's hair is brown and curly and her eyes are either blue or green. Around her neck she wears an orange silk scarf that is tied in a pretty bow. An image flashes through my mind where I am eating a slice of blueberry pie and kissing her on the mouth.

"I'll save you a slice," she says pleasantly, coquettishly.

It's warm outside. It's going to be summer soon. I unlock my bicycle from the lamppost, and the thick chain bangs fiercely against the steel. A coworker walks by holding a potted plant.

"Look at Martha's rubber tree," he says.

Down Forty-second Street I ride, past the library, past the pizza shop, past Bryant Park that's filled with office workers eating lunch. The iron fencing is gone now, as are the high hedges, as are the drug dealers and prostitutes. There is no man being terrorized with sticks, there is no lost little boy standing on the corner. People sit on the plush green grass ringed by flowers. A sign announcing free knitting classes in the park on Wednesday evenings completes the end of an era.

When I turn down Seventh Avenue, a wind swirls behind me and I pick up speed like a boat on a lake. Traffic is thick, but I dodge and weave between the cars. I'm adept at navigating this city. I've ridden all over it. Once as far as Coney Island. Once to Yonkers.

At Twenty-eighth Street, the traffic thins considerably and I am able to ride without impediment or peril. I can see all the way down into the Village. A long row of green traffic lights unfolds before me. How beautiful the city looks. How peaceful. This city that I love and never want to leave again.

At the audition I give my head shot and résumé to a disinterested elderly woman. She tells me to stand against the wall so she can take a Polaroid of me. I try to smile, but I'm terrible at smiling on demand. The result is something in between, which I'm sure looks unflattering. I want to ask her if she'll take another one, but before I can, she staples the photograph to my résumé and tells me to take a seat.

There are actors and actresses here for other auditions. I watch them come and go. They are attractive and glamorous, carrying themselves as if they are already stars. When they smile for the Polaroid, they smile broadly. When they exit, it is with a flourish. Even the disinterested woman finds them enthralling. Eventually a door opens and a pretty woman about my age appears in the doorway and loudly mispronounces my name.

"Did I get it right?" she winces.

"Don't worry," I say, "no one does."

"I'm sorry," she says. And she does seem sorry. I hope that I have used this opportunity to come across as charming and easygoing.

In the room she asks me to stand in front of a video camera while she looks over my meaningless résumé.

"It looks great," she says anyway.

Then she presses a button and the room is filled with Will Smith singing his hit song "Gettin' Jiggy wit It." She presses another button and the room goes quiet.

"Do you know that song?" she asks.

"I love that song," I say with enthusiasm. I want her to know I am enthusiastic.

"Great!" she says. Her enthusiasm matches mine. And

she briefly explains that such-and-such company is making a music video of "Gettin' Jiggy wit It," which will spoof the original music video of "Gettin' Jiggy wit It."

We both laugh at the clever idea.

Then she says, "When I press play, could you just dance along to the music?"

"Sure!" The enthusiasm again.

"And when the chorus kicks in, if you could just sing along."

"Sure!"

"Oh," as if an afterthought, "if you could do that with an accent . . ."

"Sure," but the enthusiasm is gone now. Despondency spreads across my face. I can feel it spreading. I must recover quickly or all is lost. "What kind of accent are you looking for?" I say spiritedly.

"Well," she says, pretending to mull the possibilities, "how about Middle Eastern?"

I understand the implication. It will be funny to see a Middle Eastern person singing a rap song, absurd and clownish. I'd probably laugh if I saw it too. However, I don't want to be the one doing it. This is the problem with my acting career. I'm mostly called to audition for roles like deli owner, taxi driver, and "Third World despot." Friends always tell me I look somewhere between Italian and Greek, but it doesn't really matter what I look like, my name has firmly ensconced me in a world of stereotypes. "Well, you're not quite right for the role of homeowner," a producer once told me, "but we do have *deli* owner." Often I've thought about changing my name. How simple life would be if I became a Harris. Sam Harris. Maybe Stan Harris. My uncle saw the importance of this when, at the start of his writing career, he changed his name from Finkelstein. *Harris* effectively buried the Jew. And my mother followed suit shortly thereafter.

But I can't do it. I've clung to this gigantic name my whole life. It was the only connection I had to my father when I was a little boy. In many ways it's the only connection I have to him now. We are the last remaining Sayrafiezadehs in the United States, as my brother and sister have long ago changed their name. There's irony in this.

So I do what the casting director wants and exactly how she wants it. I dance wildly out of rhythm because I know it looks buffoonish, and when the chorus kicks in I sing far off-key, with an accent that is some melding of my father and the Indian man who works at the coffee shop across from work. It is anything but authentic. The casting director doesn't seem to notice or care. She is standing behind the video camera, smiling with encouragement as this is recorded for eternity. I am ashamed and fatigued. What would my father say if he could see me now? "Look what the capitalists are making you do." That's what he would say.

Back at the office, I sit on my soft chair and look at my computer screen filled with pictures of outdoor patio furniture on the porch, in the garden, by the pool. I have a headache, but the images are soothing. I would like to be there by the pool.

"Hey, Saïd," I hear Karen say behind me.

"Don't worry," I say, "I promise I'll have them finished by the end of the day."

And suddenly she is standing next to me, very close, her hip dangerously close to my elbow. I look up and see her pretty face and her orange scarf and her eyes that are either blue or green. In her hand she is holding a slice of blueberry pie.

11

MY UNCLE'S PRESENCE HUNG IN the background of my life in Pittsburgh, a smudgy figure who never fully took shape and never fully disappeared. We had moved to Pittsburgh because he had suggested we do so, but I don't really know how much we ever benefited from him or his suggestion. I felt humiliated each time I entered his enormous house and sat down at his enormous dining-room table that reached up to my neck like I was standing in the deepest end of the swimming pool. Sitting across from me would be my cousin Henry, who, always handsome and self-possessed, looked at ease eating out of a bowl that matched the plate that matched the cup, fearlessly helping himself to seconds and thirds. How had he come by such good fortune? How had I not? When the meal was done, I would crawl onto the lush carpeting like an animal in search of a place to sleep and I would watch my uncle place log after log into the fireplace as he chatted with my mother about their own childhood and their own parents, neither of whom I had ever known. Later on I might go out to the backyard with Henry to play catch or down into the basement and watch his train choo-choo around the miniature village. It was always inconceivable to me that no part of this home belonged to me and that soon I would be asked to leave. I despised them for this. They were rich asses, after all, and I blamed them for what I did not have. My cousin slept in a sovereign bedroom that his parents did not need to traverse in order to reach the bathroom, while my mother and I lived in a one-bedroom apartment, with me in the bedroom and my mother in the living room sleeping on a twin bed that doubled, without alteration of any sort, as a couch in the daylight hours. Each morning I would wake to the sounds of her using the toilet just a few feet away from me. I could only guess at what would befall my uncle and cousin—and their house—when the revolution finally arrived, and there was some half-empty satisfaction in that.

And too soon, much too soon, my cousin would flick the switch and the train would come to a halt and the village would go dark and we would ascend to the living room, where the fire was now just embers. My mother and I would gather our belongings and pile into the backseat of my uncle's light-blue Mercedes, where he would commence to drive us home, a mere fifteen minutes away, but it always felt like we were being shepherded to the border.

"Did you enjoy yourself this evening, Saïd?" my uncle would ask.

Once back in my apartment I would become overwrought by how cramped everything seemed, how dingy, dingier than before even, the walls, the rugs, the furniture. Now, though, I turned the frustration inward, blaming and punishing myself. I tidied and straightened and organized, again and again, all my shoes in a row, all my clothes folded precisely. In the shower, I would stand beneath the hot water, letting it cascade over my skin, scalding it, believing that the water was disinfecting me and that when I finally stepped from the tub, hot and flushed, something would be transformed. It would be months before I visited my uncle again, and while there was relief in knowing this, his presence remained inescapable in the books that lined our bookcase. It was the books in the end that really defined him for me, that made him flesh. Not what was written inside them—I had never read any—but the fact that my mother had taken the time to place them side by side on an entire shelf, an act of tribute. Many, many books. Dusty and musty and worn. The result of effort, of labor, a testament to what could be accomplished if one wanted to accomplish something. *Twentyone Twice*; *Mark the Glove Boy or, The Last Days of Richard Nixon*; *The Goy; Killing Everybody*. Two copies of *Bang the Drum Slowly*, one hardcover and one soft. His was the life my mother had dreamed of living until that autumn day years earlier when she had taken a stroll through the University of Minnesota with her husband and two children and stopped for a moment, just a moment, to hear about a newspaper called *The Militant. Trumpet to the World*; *City of Discontent*; *The Southpaw*; *A Ticket for a Seamstitch*; *Something About a Soldier*; *Wake Up, Stupid*; *Friedman & Son*. Each one given as gifts to my mother, some even with handwritten inscriptions in them, if I ever dared look. *Twentyone Twice, For Martha and Mahmoud. January 1967.*

But as many books as my uncle had written and my mother had saved, the real author of our bookcase was Pathfinder Press. Lining the shelves over and around Mark Harris, answering his output by dwarfing it, belittling it, were books by Marx (for a long time I confused *Marx* with *Mark's*), Engels,

Lenin, Trotsky, Barnes—the parents and their offspring, the big and the small. *The Origins of Materialism*; *The Origin of the Family, Private Property, and the State*; *Empiricism and Its Evolution: A Marxist View*; *James P. Cannon and the Early Years of American Communism*; *The First Five Years of the Communist International*; *The First Ten Years of American Communism*; *History of American Trotskyism, 1928–38*; *Defense Policies and Principles of the Socialist Workers Party*; *America's Road to Socialism*; *Women and the Family*; *Teamster Rebellion*; *Teamster Power*; *Teamster Politics*; *Teamster Bureaucracy*; *Che Guevara Talks to Young People*.

I would look at these titles sometimes when I was home alone and I would wonder what they meant and what was inside. When I opened them to see if there might be pictures to entertain me, I discovered that the covers, the spines, the pages were still stiff and fresh. The books had barely been touched by my mother, barely read. The titles were powerful enough; they were all you needed to know about what the books contained. You did not need to venture within.

Something sad had happened in the past—that is what the titles conveyed. Something sad, something lost. *The Prophet Unarmed*; *The Prophet Outcast*; *The Revolution Betrayed*; *Lenin's Final Fight*. All that had been achieved by the Russian Revolution, by such monumental work, had come unraveled in 1924 with the death of Lenin. That unhappy moment that set in motion Stalin's ascendancy and Trotsky's demise. If only the ailing Lenin had been able to pass the torch to Trotsky, things would be different now, things would be their opposite. There had been a chance for peace and plenty, but that was several generations ago, and now we, the descendants, were stuck, and it was up to us to unstick ourselves. It was possible but it would take all our dedication, all our effort. It remained to be seen if we were up to the task. Not we meaning humanity; not we meaning the workers; we meaning the members of the Socialist Workers Party. The very future of the world depended on us.

12

EVERY FRIDAY AND SUNDAY NIGHT of my childhood was re-served expressly for the Socialist Workers Party. Friday night a forum was held that was open to the public, and where party members, or an invited guest, would speak on a cur-rent political event like the grape boycott or desegregation busing or the Equal Rights Amendment. Sunday nights were "branch meetings" for comrades only and pertained to the management and strategy of the Socialist Workers Party it-self. This is not to imply that these were the only evenings of political activity. There were also "plant-gate sales," i.e., sell-ing *The Militant* at the gates of factories during shift changes; "paste-ups," i.e., illegally pasting posters of upcoming events on walls and lampposts—done late at night to avoid being spotted by the police; the occasional party to celebrate an ac-complishment of some sort; conferences; rallies; etc.

When I was very young and still living in Brooklyn, my mother would almost always bring me along with her to these Friday and Sunday night meetings. In the early evening we would catch the subway into lower Manhattan, where we would then ride a wobbly elevator to the eighth floor of an old office building. Upon entering the meeting hall, I would instantly be greeted by a roomful of comrades.

"How's the little revolutionary doing tonight?" they would call out.

When it was time for the meeting to begin, I would snuggle down beside my mother and listen as the room fell silent and somber. The only sound was my mother's encumbered, asthmatic breathing amid the clouds of cigarette smoke passing above our heads. And then out of the void would come the rustling of the first comrade's shoes as they approached the podium. "Good evening, comrades," they would say into the microphone, and the voice would boom over me. I was warmed by the voice. Lulled by it. I never really understood what it was saying, of course, but I could follow it like a film in a foreign language, tracking the cadence if not the meaning. At a very early age I became expert at knowing when a speech was reaching its climax or when applause was being elicited or when a question from the floor was opening up an entirely new path of discussion. There was always a learned confidence in the speaker's voice, a complete understanding of why the world worked the way it worked, and this was heartening to me. It proved that it was possible to make order out of chaos. And since my mother never directly addressed the actual content of our existence, never ventured to acknowledge those things that by their very absence resounded so loudly each day, there was something alluring about being in the presence of men and women who had committed their lives to uncovering the hidden, unspoken secrets of the world. Secrets that had been buried by the sediment of years and that, if not for the mighty effort of the comrades—including my mother—would be gone forever.

When the voice was done, another voice would take its place, picking up where the previous voice had ended. As evening turned into night, and night turned into late night, I would grow drowsy and begin to slump and fade. My mother would lay me down across a row of empty folding chairs, her jacket over me, and I would drift off to sleep listening to the sound of questions asked, points raised, matters discussed, secrets revealed.

I suppose I was not the best companion to have. Once, in the middle of a dream, I rolled and fell off the folding chairs, crashing onto the floor and bringing the proceedings to a halt. Another time, during a voice vote, I inexplicably shouted out "nay," deeply embarrassing myself and my mother. To solve the problem, my mother took to confining me to the back rooms, where, among the piles of that week's *Militant* and still within easy range of the amplified voice, I would pass the time playing with office supplies. There was a brief period when a little nameless girl would also attend the meetings, and together we would create entire adventures with rubber bands and staplers. On one occasion she was scolded for painting her nails using a bottle of Wite-Out and on another for boldly marching up to the podium and interrupting her father, who was in the middle of giving a report. After that she was seen no more.

At some point my mother came to the conclusion that it would be better if I also didn't attend these meetings so regularly and instead remained home alone. So, aside from an occasional event here and there, I was relegated to the apartment on those Friday and Sunday nights. It did not go well in the beginning. I once woke in the middle of the night to discover that my mother had still not come home. From room to room I scurried, calling out to her—"Where are you, Ma?"—living room to bedroom, bathroom to kitchen, quicker and quicker, thinking that I must have surely overlooked the obvious and would suddenly see her sitting there. Eventually I gave up the hunt and collapsed on the living-room floor, clutching my coloring book to my chest like a security blanket. That is how my mother found me—who knows how many hours later—when she finally came through the front door, her knapsack on her back and a perplexed expression on her face.

"Why aren't you asleep?"

By the time I arrived in Pittsburgh, I had learned how to sleep through the night without incident. In my solitary waking hours, though, I was frightened by everything—the plunks and clinks of the building, the sound of footsteps in the hallway, the thought that my mother this time might not return at all. The shadows cast by furniture were lurking men; the sound of a neighbor's toilet was the doorknob being jiggled; car headlights reflecting on the walls were flames; a fly was a cockroach; a cockroach was a rat. All was possible.

My mother had posted the number of the party headquarters by the phone in case of emergency, but it served only as a constant flashing reminder that danger was an ever-present possibility and that I would be helpless in the face of it. Everything I did while she was away went toward constructing an alternate reality, one of peace and tranquillity. The stories I chose to read were expunged of conflict. The games I invented were of the lightest fare, of the happiest people, of the brightest colors. The power of these modes of entertainment to distract me was temporary, and the only thing that could keep the terror fully at bay was our thirteen-inch black-and-white television set. This was forbidden to me except for special occasions, but in my mother's absence I would linger for hours in front of it, counting among my many friends the Jeffersons, the Bunkers, the Newharts. As the evening wore on, though, these programs were replaced by hour-long dramas that dismayed me with their heavier scenarios. Programs like *The Incredible Hulk,* or *Fantasy Island,* or *That's Incredible!* where I once watched as a man, in the interest of science, dove into a swimming pool with twenty-pound weights attached to his wrists and ankles, so that re-searchers could monitor the effects of drowning on a human being. I was petrified by this nightmarish content, but I would forgo my bedtime and continue watching. The television set, no matter how terrifying it might become, was always a more palatable alternative than the reality that encircled me.

It was during one of these dark nights that my uncle's movie happened to come on. I had never seen it before. *Bang the Drum Slowly,* the television read. *Screenplay by Mark Harris. Based upon his novel.*

Our television was black and white, but my uncle's name glowed in yellow light. I pictured his house instantly, the soft carpeting, the staircase, the painting of the massive chocolate bar that hung in the landing of that staircase. As the opening credits rolled, two baseball players jogged silently side by side in an empty baseball stadium, towels around their necks. The slowest, saddest music played in the background, all flutes and violins, indicating that whatever things lay ahead for these men would not be good things. And sure enough, the scene switched from the baseball stadium to the front of a hospital, where the men, now dressed in ties and carrying luggage, exited through the front doors, bidding farewell to a doctor, the violins still going.

I sat in my pajamas and watched the story unfold. The plot was thick and tiring and I lost my way in the adult innuendo. I had been expecting a movie about baseball; instead, it was about illness. A man was dying and another man was trying to keep it a secret. From time to time I thought of changing the channel, but it was my uncle's movie and I felt to do so would be ungenerous. And so I watched as the brooding sadness wound around me, entrapping me. A man raced through a hotel in the middle of the night in search of a doctor. Another man collapsed on the baseball field. Another shot a gun in drunken triumph. And finally, many hours after it had begun, the dying baseball player stood with his suitcase, about to board an airplane.

"Thanks for everything, Author," he said, smiling at his good friend. "I'll be back in the spring. I'll be in shape. You'll see."

And I understood, as each of them did, that these were just words and that he would soon be dead.

"Yeah," said the other man, "I'll see you then."

And a few minutes later the movie was over. It was late. It was past my bedtime. The credits rolled. I waited for my uncle's name to appear one more time, but it did not. I turned off the television and was quickly released back into the world of the apartment. The silence rushed into me, clogging my ears. I turned the light on in my bedroom before I turned the light off in the living room, trying to navigate my way into sleep in as little darkness as possible. And so I did. Lying next to my teddy bears and dreaming, I don't know of what, until some moment when I sensed my mother's presence in my bedroom, leaning over me in the blackness, kissing me on the forehead, the smell of cigarette smoke clinging to her clothes.

Over time my mother began to grow concerned with the unhealthy impact of such excessive television-watching on a young mind. It would destroy my intellect, she said. It would turn my brain to mush. "It's a boob tube, Saïd." I was instructed to read, write, or draw while she was away. I protested. She insisted. I disobeyed. She demanded. I would open a book and pretend to be engrossed as she readied herself to depart, but as soon as she was out of earshot I would turn on the television. She caught on to this, tiptoeing back up the stairwell and pressing her ear against the door, then bursting in like a cop in a cop show. When I denied my crime, she would feel the back of the set as if checking a feverish forehead.

"Why is it hot?"

"The light from the lamp must have made it hot."

She tried being angry with me, but I could not be swayed by admonishment. She would then affect disappointment, hoping that would cause my conscience to kick in. It did not.

As fate would have it, one day she discovered that she could remove the electrical cord from the back of the television set. Now, an hour or two prior to her leaving, she would unplug the cord and hide it. This did not elicit the effect she desired either. As soon as she was gone, I would begin to forage for the missing cord. It was not such a terrible predicament to be in; the search kept me occupied, and I was able to fix my mind on a goal and pursue it with relentless fervor. Loneliness, anger, fright, boredom were all submerged. It was an attainable goal too; the cord was somewhere between the walls of our tiny apartment, and although there were quite a number of options of where it might be, the options nonetheless were finite. I rifled through everything like a seasoned burglar—her panty drawer, her bra drawer, her diary drawer, her jar of keepsakes. Nothing was sacred, and I always found the cord in the end.

Weeks of treasure hunts went by. Then months went by. Then a year. I became accustomed to the hunt, evolving from dread at my mother's departures to anticipation of them as opportunities to indulge in the pursuit, with the prize being the terrible elixir of situation comedy. I would plot my viewing days in advance. If for some reason or other a meeting had been canceled or rescheduled and my mother stayed home, I would wallow in disappointment and frustration.

Eventually my mother had removed the cord so many times that it no longer stayed firmly connected to the set but would, in the middle of a program, fall straight out of the back. The flood of silent reality would propel me from my chair like a sprinter at the gun. The more I had to push the cord into the set, the more compromised it became, so that in the end I came to a well-reasoned childish conclusion that wetting the end of it would cause it to stick firmly in place, like a postage stamp to an envelope. With the electrical cord still plugged into the wall, I would put my mouth on the other end of it and lick, then lick again, then place it back into the television set and continue comfortably with my viewing.

Then early one Sunday evening when I was probably about ten years old, I watched in utter horror as my mother, in the somber ritual of a robed priest at Mass, unplugged the cord from the electrical outlet, removed it from the back of the television set, unzipped her knapsack, placed it inside, and left for her meeting. I listened to the key turn in the lock and her footsteps first in the hallway, then down the stairs, *clip clip clip,* and then gone. The war was over. My mother had won. The night stretched before me interminably. My punishment was imprisonment. A life sentence.

Just a few blocks from where my mother and I lived was a pizza shop called "Uncle Charlie's." It was a small, dim place that had a video game and a pinball machine. The pinball machine appealed to a previous generation to which I did not belong. The video game, however, was always crowded with boys eagerly watching the action like gamblers at a cockfight. On afternoons I would insinuate myself among the older, stronger boys and watch them play. There was a masculinity to what they could accomplish, deftly reaching levels the younger boys could only aspire to.

I was horrible at the game. I never fully understood the rules. I panicked quickly under pressure. I was too deliberate at aiming at the enemy spaceships. There was gratitude when it was over, like returning to the waking world from a horrible dream. Then I would step back and let the older boys take the reins.

The night my mother exited with the television cord, it occurred to me that, unlike a prisoner, I was actually free to go to Uncle Charlie's if I wanted. I withdrew a lone dollar bill from my dresser drawer and looked at it. What evidence would there be that I had ever left the apartment? Not a trace.

At the present, Uncle Charlie's was owned by an overweight man with black hair and bushy eyebrows whose name was Joel but whom everyone called Charlie. He was eating a slice of pizza when I entered. (I envied the infinite supply of pizza that was afforded him.) The place was empty. The floor had been swept clean, the small tables cleared of debris. The clock on the wall read 8:50. I was prepared for him to ask why I was out at this late hour, but he did not. With disinterest, he gave me four quarters for my dollar. I dropped a coin through the slot of the game. The machine beat out its drum-drum music as the enemy spacecraft flew in to attack. I fired at them, bullet after bullet, and the spaceships disintegrated on impact. It was satisfying to destroy. And in my mind, I began to play a different game than the one that was depicted. I imagined my spaceship was a communist spaceship and the enemy spaceships were the spaceships of the capitalists. The stakes of this duel energized me. On level one, I soundly defeated capitalism. And on level two as well. And then on three. As each subsequent level of the video game appeared on the screen, all I had killed before reappeared to be killed again, and each time there were more of them and they were faster and more resilient, and each time I was up to the task. I thought of the older boys and their video-game athleticism, and I wondered what they would think of me now. My left hand ached from clutching the joystick, and the tips of the fingers on my right hand were numb from pounding away furiously at the yellow button that dispensed my bullets. My weapons were the weapons of Marx, Engels, Trotsky, Jack Barnes. And the ships that came to kill me were piloted by Jimmy Carter, Andrew Carnegie, the "rich asses," and Uncle Charlie himself. Eventually there was no chance whatsoever, the speed of the machine had grown exponentially, and in the midst of an impossible amount of capitalist spaceships I went down in flames.

I stood at the machine, dazed, spent, watching as it ranked me and invited me to add my initials. I had three quarters left. It was 9:20. I put another quarter in. I made a careless mistake and was killed on the first screen. It was 9:22. I put another quarter in. I was killed on the second screen. I slapped the side of the machine. "Hey, you!" Uncle Charlie cried out. I put another quarter in. I played with resignation, with defeat. "If I lose, I lose because I do not even care enough about you to try to win." I lost. I had no more quarters. I looked at the floor for a possible stray. The floor had been swept clean. I was humiliated by my need. I felt sudden rage at the boys who always seemed in possession of an endless supply of quarters. The rage was replaced by sadness. It would be a long time before I came by another dollar. I wanted it back. I wanted to undo it.

There was not a soul on the street. It was very dark now, very empty. Suddenly I understood how odd it was for a little boy to be outside in the streets alone at a time of night like this. I was like someone who has ventured far out into a driving rainstorm before realizing that it is in fact a hurricane. I took the long, most well-lit way home, walking slowly, hoping to affect an air of nonchalance that would dissuade a predator. With relief I entered the apartment building and walked the two flights of stairs to my floor. Perhaps my mother's meeting had let out early and she was now home, frightened, irritated, waiting to chastise me for my senselessness. "Where have you been, Saïd!" I unlocked the door and the stillness of the apartment washed over me.

On top of the bookcase my mother kept a little brown sugar jar that she used for storing spare cash. It was always filled with coins and crumpled-up bills. When I had first discovered the jar, years earlier, it seemed miraculous to me. My mother had told me that the jar was Persian, so I had come to associate the jar and the money with my father, imagining that he had given it to my mother as a sort of onetime alimony payment when he left. That night, I unscrewed the lid and took out a dollar. I felt as if I was crossing an invisible barrier, but I could not make out the person crossing it.

I went out into the night again. This time without deliberation. The novelty of the experience had worn off. It was completely dark, but I was not frightened by the darkness. Uncle Charlie was noisily sipping a Coke through a straw when I entered. He didn't ask how I had come by another dollar. He gave me change. I played hard; I lost quickly. The clock read 10:12. There was a pinching in my elbow from the strain of gripping the joystick so tightly. I wanted to crush something in my hands. I had to pee badly, and the sensation incited me. The shortcut to my home was through an alley-way. It was jet-black, but as a punishment for having spent and for having lost, I walked through it anyway. There was a recklessness to it that I deserved. I fantasized about being accosted by the shadows. I had homework to do, but it was too late to do it now. I had wasted the night. I wanted the night back. The only thing that could alleviate this discomfort, that could redeem me, that could let me pee, was to play the video game again. I entered the apartment. The stillness. I did not hesitate; I went straight for the brown sugar jar.

13

I AM GREETED AT THE front entrance of the Iranian restaurant by a man I presume to be Iranian. He is wearing a shirt and tie, and he says to me with disturbing élan, "Table for one, sir?"

"No," I say, "I'm supposed to be meeting someone here."

"Please have a look," he says, bending slightly at the waist and gesturing at the restaurant with a wide sweep of his arm, as if he is a doorman and I am the tenant.

The restaurant is small, and with the exception of an older couple sitting at a table, it is without patrons. Although I can plainly see that my father has not yet arrived, I continue to stand there, taking in the confines, looking from table to table in case I have overlooked the obvious. Then I walk back past the Iranian man, who says, "Thank you, sir," as if I have done him a great service.

Tonight's dinner with my father is something of a thirtieth-birthday celebration for me. My thirtieth birthday was six months ago. We had been planning to get together, until an important and unexpected event arose: a meeting. President Clinton had just begun a four-day bombing of Iraq under what was known as Operation Desert Fox, and in response the Socialist Workers Party called an emergency meeting to map out a strategy on how the working class should best respond.

"We will have to do this another time," my father had said

to me over the phone. The distant gravity of his voice—as if he were looking over important documents as we spoke—gave the impression that the upcoming meeting would have an impact on global affairs. I had agreed to reschedule immediately and without objection; to do otherwise would have made me seem crass and uncaring regarding the suffering of others. A few weeks later I received a leaflet in the mail that was advertising the latest issue of the Socialist Workers Party's annual journal, *New International: A Magazine of Marxist Politics and Theory.* There was no note included with the leaflet, but I assumed it had been sent by my father. This latest issue of *New International* was written by Jack Barnes and was entitled "The Opening Guns of World War III." It had originally been published seven years earlier after the first Gulf War but was now being reissued as a "special war issue." The cover showed a line of American tanks parked in the desert. Sitting atop the tanks were soldiers looking through binoculars, waiting for the order to begin their assault.

The journal was priced at twelve dollars but was being offered at a ten percent discount. I saved the leaflet for a while, thinking that I would buy it, or that I *should* buy it, but I never did. A month passed. Two months passed. I thought of calling my father, but is it poor etiquette to request a birthday dinner for oneself? In my moment of indecision, other political events occurred, then others, crowding in tightly on one another and presumably occupying my father in planning and strategy. In February, Amadou Diallo, poor, black, and unarmed, was shot nineteen times by New York City police officers, and Socialist Workers Party forums were quickly planned. Then spring came and NATO began bombing Serbia. STOP THE IMPERIALIST BOMBING OF YUGO-SLAVIA! read the headline of an issue of *The Militant*. And after that my father flew off to the Tehran book fair that he has attended each year for many years, acting as the party's Persian-language editor for Pathfinder Press. And after that I turned thirty and a half.

Then one day, apropos of nothing, the phone rang.

"Sidsky!" my father cried out, his voice full of immense cheer, like a sailor who has survived rough seas and has finally made it back to shore into the arms of those who have been waiting for him. In that single word—*Sidsky!*—all was instantly forgiven by me, or forgotten, and that is how I find myself standing in front of an Iranian restaurant in the Garment District waiting for my father.

What if, while I was inside the restaurant, my father arrived outside and then, seeing that I was not there, did not think to look inside and simply decided that I came and went, and so he decided to leave? "You weren't there, Sidsky . . ."

I make my way to the corner, past men pulling racks of wedding dresses, and look in the direction of the subway station, but there is no sign of a retreating man who resembles my father. What if he has not taken the subway at all and is coming from another direction entirely? I hurry the other way. And, sure enough, here he comes from the far end of the block, my father, just as I remember him, his gait long and purposeful.

No, it is not my father but a man who looks like my father. Suddenly I see him everywhere, as if a great wind has gathered up all the approximations of my father in New York City and blown them in my direction. There is one who dresses exactly as my father would dress, and another who is bald but not as handsome, and another who is handsome but without glasses. It occurs to me that I was a fool to ever leave my post in front of the restaurant. So I hurry back, determined to stand outside without interruption, but it now behooves me to again go inside and see if my father has entered and taken a table for two.

And from out of the maelstrom comes a voice I would recognize anywhere: "Hello, Sidsky."

I turn and there he is, smiling widely, his face a study in calm.

"Pop," I shout as if I am faraway down the street. "I was getting worried, Pop." There is irritation in my voice, and I regret the irritation.

"Am I late?" he says with concern. Then he pulls back his sleeve and checks his watch. "No, Sidsky," he says, "I am on time."

It doesn't matter anymore. All that has come before recedes into faint outlines and I put my arms out to hug him, to greet him properly, but as I do I can see him stiffen slightly, like an ironing board put upright, and he extends his hand for me to shake. I have no choice but to take it. My hand is thin and his hand is permanently puffy, swollen, the hand of marshmallows. "From those Tehran winters," he will say, "when I was too poor to buy gloves." We shake firmly like acquaintances, acquaintances who are friendly toward each other.

If my father has aged since the last time I saw him, it is imperceptible. He has neither lost nor gained weight, and he is dressed as he is always dressed, which is to say in the attire of a mathematics professor: a blue tie, a white shirt—his big belly straining against the buttons—a pen in his pocket, a small notepad behind the pen, black slacks, black shoes. He looks somewhere between rich and poor and he smells faintly of BO, affecting without being repellent. My father has a round, pleasant face, and he looks at me from behind round, wire-rimmed glasses. "Ask me a question," his face seems to say, "and I will tell you an answer." I wish there was a question I could think of, because there is something truly inviting about him, like a bear, hearty, robust, comforting. Every time I see him he seems to be full of energy and zest. He stays up late, he wakes up early, he doesn't complain. He seems never worried, anxious, ill at ease, plagued by the thought of things to come. He believes that the world is quickly spiraling downward, of course, that poverty is unresolvable, that wars are constant, but these thoughts do not distress him in the way they distressed my mother and me. Instead, he is invigorated by them. The revolution will come, certainly, and when it does, all will be well. Until then there is work to be done, food to be eaten, wine to be drunk, and sex to be had. I am sure my father will live to be a hundred.

The only thing that unhinges his outward appearance as a scholar is that sitting atop his bald head is a black baseball cap with white lettering that reads *International Brotherhood of Electrical Workers*. I have never seen my father wearing a baseball cap before, and I find its presence disquieting. It stands out in such sharp relief from the rest of his attire that it may as well be lit by neon lights. It is well worn and cocked just slightly to the side, giving him a rakish quality that undermines his obvious intellectual demeanor, like he is an urchin from another era who has come out of an alleyway to beg for food. Perhaps he was given this cap by a member of the International Brotherhood of Electrical Workers when he was selling copies of *The Militant* on their picket line. "It was given to me as an act of solidarity," my father might say. Or for that matter he might say that he refused the worker's gift and instead paid for it with his own money, and that *this* act was an act of solidarity. That is a question I suppose I could ask, but I know that we are in for a long evening of politics and it does not make sense to begin any sooner than we need to. Besides, I am concerned that if I draw attention to the cap he will think the cap is resonant and proudly leave it on in the restaurant, which to my way of thinking would be highly inappropriate. And if I were to say this aloud to him, "Pop, I think you should take the hat off," he would then most likely perceive this as a direct attack on the International Brotherhood of Electrical Workers and on unionism in general. It is best to hold my tongue.

Lenin also wore a cap of a strikingly similar nature, rough and floppy and somewhat whimsical. His cap, though, was purchased when he was in Stockholm on the eve of the revolution and was favored not by the proletariat but by painters of the early twentieth century. He can be seen wearing the hat in a photo from 1919 where he converses amiably with Trotsky and Kamenev. It is also there, squeezed in his right hand, while he leans over the podium in Sverdlov Square in Moscow, exhorting the soldiers of the Red Army before they depart for the Polish front. Or there it is, back on his head when he is at Gorki, sitting in a wheelchair, his health rapidly failing, the end near, Stalin waiting in the wings. Lenin's cap contradicted his suit and tie, contradicted his appearance as an intellectual, and set him apart from other revolutionaries of the time, in much the same way that my father's cap sets him apart. I believe that this is the point. Look at me, I am a math professor, yes, but my allegiance is with those who labor with their hands, those who organize, those who struggle, those who toil. Look at me, I am not the man you think I am but something else, something in the space between professor and electrical worker—a third thing altogether. *Ask me a question.*

Easier to ignore, but no less disconcerting, is that hanging from one of my father's shoulders is the strap of a blue knapsack. They are ubiquitous accoutrements for comrades in the Socialist Workers Party, these knapsacks. My mother carried hers every time she left home. Contained inside were all the tools necessary for revolutionary action: the latest copies of *The Militant,* leaflets for upcoming forums or demonstrations, a roll of tape, a stapler, a box of staples, another roll of tape. We were like hikers, she and I, ascending the mountain of revolution. Often on the way to somewhere my mother would stop abruptly in front of a lamppost or telephone pole, kneel on the concrete, unzip her knapsack, and remove a leaflet that might say something like: *U.S. out of El Salvador! March on Washington!* on such and such date, with a paragraph or so summarizing the road that lay ahead for working people living under an imperialist government that was squeezing them tighter and tighter. I would stop beside my mother and stand to the side, observing the simple sequence of her stooping over her knapsack on the sidewalk, nearly wrestling with it, digging around for the leaflet, righting herself, pounding the stapler into the telephone pole—*bang, bang, bang.* It must be pressed with great force so the wind did not take it away. People passing by would glance at my mother, then at the leaflet, then at me. I was always deathly embarrassed by this. I felt as if my clothes had been removed. No one ever stopped to read what the leaflet said, no one ever said, "I agree, tell me more," no one ever even said, "I disagree." What was of great consequence to us was of no consequence to them.

"Let's eat," my father says. "Shall we eat? I'm getting hungry."

"Sure, Pop," I say. "I'm hungry too."

The two of us enter the restaurant and stand waiting for the man in the tie while he seats another table, bowing before them, smiling, thanking. Then he comes toward us.

"Hello," he says. I do not think he remembers me. "Two for dinner?"

"Yes," my father says.

"Please," he says, and he bows slightly and my father bows slightly, and then he ushers us to a table near the back.

The restaurant is carpeted and has low romantic lighting and white linen tablecloths. On each table there is a tiny vase with a single daisy so precise in its detail that it is impossible to discern whether it is real or fake. The door has been propped open to allow a breeze to blow over the patrons. The sounds of the Garment District drift in from the street. A busboy arrives at our table and lights the votive candle. My father smiles and waves his finger over the flame. In the darkness of the restaurant, his black cap seems to have disappeared, but the white words of *International Brotherhood of Electrical Workers* look like they are floating and dancing above his head.

"Hey, Pop," I offer tentatively, "maybe you should take the cap off."

"What?" he says with alarm. And then: "Oh, yes!" And he removes it from his head and stuffs it into his blue knapsack. Just like that the matter is settled.

The waitress appears at our table. She does not look Iranian. I think she may be Chinese. She is young and pretty, though her skin seems nearly drained of pigment from too many nocturnal shifts shepherding food. She speaks shyly and with an accent, forcing us to lean in to decipher her words.

"May I start you off with something to drink?" she asks.

"May I start you off with something to drink," my father repeats to himself, mulling over the sentence for a moment like he wasn't expecting the question but appreciates its grammatical construction. Then he asks proudly, "What kind of house wine do you have?"

"We have chardonnay," the waitress begins. "We have—"

"Chardonnay! Chardonnay sounds good!" He looks at

me. "Does chardonnay sound good, Sidsky? If I order some chardonnay, will you have a glass with me?"

"Sure, Pop," I say.

"Do you hear that? The birthday boy will have a glass of chardonnay with me. Therefore, I think we are going to need more than just a single wineglass." My father smiles at the waitress as if he has said something clever. The waitress smiles back, but it's apparent she doesn't know what she's smiling about, and it's apparent my father doesn't know that she doesn't know. His smile widens.

"Let us begin," he says, "with a carafe of chardonnay."

And the waitress disappears.

My father looks at me. I look back. He says nothing. I say nothing. We could be sitting at a cafeteria table in Oberlin twenty-five years ago.

"How have you been, Sidsky?" he says eventually.

"Oh, pretty good, Pop."

"How's the acting career?"

"Not so good."

"Little by little, Sidsky."

"Thanks, Pop."

"And how is Martha Stewart doing?" The name *Martha* bounces from wall to wall, but we both ignore this.

"Not bad," I say. I think about my soft swivel chair. "She's still a billionaire."

He snickers. Then he broods.

"How about you, Pop? How have you been?"

He's been waiting for this. Without answering, he bends

and removes the troubling blue knapsack from beneath his chair and places it on his lap. Then he looks at me sharply to see if I am watching him. I assume he is going to give me a gift for my birthday, and I look away and then down at my hands, because to look directly at someone when he is preparing to give you a gift is coarse, unmannered, and above all presumptuous. He unzips the knapsack, a delicate operation, but there is some confusion over which zipper belongs to which compartment, first this way and then that, and I return to watching him like he is a magician at work and if I blink I will miss the trick. Finally, thankfully, the thing opens and he puts his hand inside, rustles around, and pulls out something and lays it on the table in front of me. I look down and *The Militant* looks up.

I see that my father has circled or underlined things in red pen, and he has written notes in the margins—*layer of peasants aligning with proletariat; effect of Stalinist decay.* There is something touching about this, something about a bright schoolboy, one with interests and aspirations, who can be seen running home with the thing he has discovered that day. My father was a smart boy, at least the way he tells it, far advanced from other children his age. I have no reason to disbelieve this one clear detail in what remains a mysterious childhood. He once described to me how, when he was a six-year-old in Tabriz, his mother would greet his playmates at the door by saying "I'm sorry, but Mahmoud cannot come out to play right now, he's reading Hafiz," referring to the fourteenth-century Persian poet and mystic. According to my father, the Western equivalent of this would be "I'm sorry, but Mahmoud cannot come out to play right now, he's reading Shakespeare." When he recounts this anecdote, he does not recount it with arrogance but with disappointment and regret, a boy looking out the bedroom window on a sunny day. He understands the pretension involved and the damaging effects of that pretension on a young person. But the legend of an exceptional mind has done nothing but grow greater with time, until it has become accepted by all who know him. And for the briefest of moments I am with my mother again, it is morning, she is making breakfast, I am playing on the floor near her, and she is saying to me regarding some conversation that is taking place inside her: "If only I could have kept up with Mahmoud's politics. I think then things might have turned out differently for me."

The waitress places a carafe of chardonnay in front of us. My father looks at her ass as she walks away. Then he looks at the carafe of chardonnay. Then he looks at me.

"This is white," he says to me.

"It's chardonnay."

"I wanted red."

"Chardonnay isn't red."

"Never?"

"I don't think so."

"Shit," he says to himself.

There's a difficult interlude while we both contemplate the ramifications. Then my father perks up. "Sidsky, have you been following the coal miners' strike?"

"No, Pop," I say, wishing I had been following it. "Actually, I haven't even heard about it."

My father nods. "The capitalist media is trying to keep it out of the news, of course," he says, remarkably without bitterness. "Very interesting the way things have developed." His accent causes him to stress the wrong syllable, so rather than *deVELoped,* it comes out as *develOPED.*

He points to *The Militant.*

NATO BOMBS KILL SERB AND ALBANIAN WORKERS, the headline announces. RIFTS GROW BETWEEN WASHINGTON, IMPERIALIST ALLIES. A photo shows a group of Chinese men and women holding a banner that reads in both Chinese and English, *Stop Murderous Bombing,* and beneath that photo is a second photo, a smaller one, of a bomb exploding spectacularly, like fireworks, on a pleasant sidewalk lined with potted pants.

"No, Sidsky, look here," and he unfolds *The Militant* and smooths it out, and sure enough, just as he has said, there is an article reporting on the coal miners' strike.

"This is the only publication where you'll be able to find out the truth," he says, as if this might be the first time I've ever seen a copy of *The Militant.* Then he says nothing. The silence makes the implication clear.

"I guess I should buy this," I say. "How much does it

cost?" It's a calculated question, of course. I know how much it costs. I ask because I want him to say: "Oh, Sidsky, come on, you don't need to pay me for it. Just take it."

"A dollar fifty," my father says. There is an undercurrent of ruthlessness in his voice that makes me certain that if I came up one dime short he would refuse me the sale.

In the penultimate apartment I lived in with my mother, we were lucky enough to have been given access to a storage bin in the basement. Nevertheless, my mother chose to keep all the hundreds of disorganized *Militant*s in a closet by the front door. It was a deep closet, deeper than any we had had before, but it was our great misfortune that the architect, whether through oversight or malice, had designed the door to open into the closet rather than out of it, which meant that the tenant was deprived of about fifty percent of the storage space. In order, therefore, to make full use of the closet, my mother simply kept the door open at all times. The first thing someone paying us a visit observed upon entering our apartment was my mother's plaid wool coat hanging from the coat hook and beneath it piles of *Militant*s running all the way to the very edge of the closet, pinning the door wide open.

I take out my wallet and withdraw some money.

"Now your perspective will be broadened," my father says happily. And I am happy too. This evening I have endeared myself to him. "The coal strike is in an anthracite region, Sidsky. Do you know what an anthracite region is?"

"No, Pop," I say. "What's an anthracite region?"

He lowers his voice and leans toward me conspiratorially. "On the surface this strike is about wages and the right to organize, but what is it really about?"

"I don't know, Pop."

He takes a breath and says with great conviction, "It is about human dignity." Each word is emphasized. Then he looks me dead in the eye like he is anticipating that human dignity will be a concept of some controversy for me and he is prepared to defend it with all he has. I think briefly about responding, just for fun, "I'm actually opposed to human dignity, Pop."

"We're having our subscription fund drive now, Sidsky. Maybe you want to think about buying a subscription. We have a twelve-issue introductory rate for ten dollars."

"I guess I should buy that." I remove more money from my wallet. My father takes it from me and places it into an empty white envelope, which he scribbles something on. Then he puts it into his blue knapsack and zips it closed.

The waitress returns to us. "Would you like to hear tonight's specials?" she asks.

My father looks up at her apologetically. "I'm very sorry," he says, "there seems to have been a mistake." His gaze moves to the carafe of chardonnay, hoping she will intuit the problem. "What I really meant to ask for, you see," he laughs shyly, "what I really wanted, you see, was red wine."

"Oh?"

"I am very sorry," my father says again. "Would you by any chance have zinfandel?"

And without continuing with the specials, the waitress swiftly removes the carafe of chardonnay and departs.

In a year or so, the Socialist Workers Party national office will be sold and relocated to just a few blocks from where we now sit in the Garment District. The idea is that it should be closer to the garment workers whom the party has identified to be central players in the upcoming working-class struggles. Meatpackers, coal miners, and airline workers are also believed to be central players. Now, however, the national office is on Charles Street in the remote West Village, where it's been since I was a little boy, both headquarters and printing press, housed in a six-story building that is, coincidentally, just five blocks from my studio apartment on Jane Street. When I ride my bicycle down the West Side Highway to Battery Park City I will pass it, sitting there facing the Hudson River next to million-dollar condos as it churns out *Militant*s and Pathfinder books. It is as plain and unadorned as every comrade's apartment. But in the late eighties the party managed to raise the impressive sum of one hundred twenty-five thousand dollars and commissioned eighty artists from twenty countries to paint a giant mural covering the entire side of the building, seventy feet high and eighty-five feet wide. There were colorful portraits of all the major players in the struggle, from Marx to Lenin to Trotsky to Che to César Chávez; every revolutionary imaginable was depicted (except Stalin and Mao), all floating around an enormous printing press that was in the midst of dispensing flowing rolls of newsprint with Castro's cumbersome maxim, "The truth must not only be the truth, it must also be told."

The mural was a huge achievement for the Socialist Workers Party and was covered each week in *The Militant* for months prior to its completion. When it was finally unveiled in the frigid cold of November 1989, it was heralded as an accomplishment born from the fruits of the Nicaraguan Revolution and dedicated to the working people of New York City and the world.

Then one night a few years later, some troublemakers threw paint on it, obscuring Castro's face, and immediately a "mural defense league" was set up. This entailed comrades sitting inside the building, watching the mural twenty-four hours a day, seven days a week. Every once in a while I'd get a phone call from my father saying that he was going to be working the midnight shift of the mural defense league and would I like to meet up for breakfast the next morning. Of course I'd say yes, and the next morning I'd wake up an hour early and walk two blocks over to La Bonbonniere on Eighth Avenue, where I would shovel in pancakes and sausage before heading off to Martha Stewart. Despite having been up all night, my father would be as energetic as always.

But the mural defense league could not defend against poor planning, and less than eight years after the mural had been completed, the colors faded and the paint peeled and the brick wall was discovered to have stress cracks and would need to be completely replaced before the entire building itself was compromised and demolished. So another one hundred thousand dollars was raised, and the faces of Marx and Lenin and Trotsky and Che and César Chávez and the words *The truth must not only be the truth, it must also be told* were pulled out brick by brick. This, too, was covered for weeks by *The Militant* and somehow was also celebrated as an accomplishment of sorts—*Honorable removal of mural*—until no trace of the mural remained, replaced instead by huge pink-colored plastic siding.

The waitress materializes beside our table. "I'm sorry," she says to my father, nodding first at the carafe of chardonnay in her hand and then at the vacant space in the center of the table. It is her turn to hope my father intuits. He does not.

"I'm sorry," she says again. Then her voice lowers to just above a whisper. "We are unable to exchange this for red wine."

My father's brown eyes stare up at her impassively as the words settle. Then he chortles as if he has just been let in on a good joke.

"I'm sorry," she repeats hopefully, "because the bottle was opened, you understand, and the bartender won't be able to resell this and—"

"Resell." My father luxuriates in the word.

The waitress smiles a reasonable smile, a no-hard-feelings smile. My father looks at me thoughtfully as if I might intercede, then he nods his head once, twice, tucks his chin against his chest like he is about to take a nap—then quickly looks up at the waitress.

"Bring the manager," my father says.

The waitress is nonplussed. *The manager?* It has quickly, unexpectedly come to this. The tiniest of tiny smiles flashes across her lips, as if this is all just poor communication that we will soon laugh about. But seeing that my father's face no longer betrays any expression of humor, she turns and hurries away, carafe in hand.

"Do you see?" His eyes are flashing in anger, as if I've participated in committing a crime. Then with great sympathy he reverses: "They've put her in a bad situation." Then to himself, despondently: "What is it to them?"

There's an awkward silence after this. My father absent-mindedly moves his finger back and forth over the candle, causing the flame to bend and dance. Then he examines the daisy in the vase and asks, "Is this real?" We adjust and readjust the silverware.

Finally, as an icebreaker, my father says, "Do you know about the history of the Garment District, Sidsky?"

"Not really," I say.

"Women," he says. "Poor women . . ." He trails off. I wait for him to go on. He moves his finger over the flame. "Have you read *The History of the Russian Revolution*, Sidsky?"

"I haven't read that, Pop." I have a flinching awareness that I have yet to answer in the affirmative this evening.

"Trotsky explains how the revolution began with the seamstresses. Do you have a copy? Next time I'll bring you a copy. Don't start with chapter one. Start with chapter six." And, as if reciting poetry, "The struggles of the seamstresses are like rising suns for the world to see."

My father knows nothing about the history of the seamstresses, of course. I'm sure he's never read a book about them, or seen a film, or gone to the library to look up an article. He just knows implicitly. Lack of knowledge is not a deterrent. My father will gladly hold forth on the largest of subjects: the social evolution of human beings since *Homo habilis*; the materialist underpinnings of ancient civilization; the French Revolution; the Cold War. He'll even talk to me about theater. The subjects he chooses are usually so vast, so breathtaking, that one can be forgiven for failing to realize how hollow the information is that he imparts. Try mentioning to him the Ottoman Empire and the way it was divided up by the victors of World War I, and he will blink back at you as if he has grown weary of discussion. "Is that so?" he will ask from far away. But in the most general of terms he can speak about imperialist oppression of the Middle East with great verve and for many hours. It's his job. He's a socialist missionary among proletariat savages, and all social intercourse presents itself as an opportunity for conversion. It doesn't matter if he himself knows the intimate details of the topics on which he expounds; his concern is with Truth. He has heard things said about the seamstresses by comrades who have heard things said by other comrades, and he can understand that they are more than likely correct, that they do not demand a major reordering of the world as he perceives it. Beyond this hearsay, though, he has never ventured independently. Such exploration would be redundant and an egregious waste of time and might, at some juncture, challenge the conclusions he has already comfortably settled upon.

And just at that moment the restaurant manager arrives at our table. I can see now that his unblemished white shirt will indicate to my father how little the man labors. It is obvious the manager is the one who has issued the dictum about the wine and is now prepared to stand behind it in the most diplomatic of ways. Behind him stands the waitress; she could be a schoolgirl visiting the principal's office with her father. In her white hand is the carafe of chardonnay, which she is clutching by the neck as if it's a chicken she's selected to strangle for supper. The manager smiles at us with that same warm, solicitous air he had when we first arrived. Now he has become the enemy.

"Because, you understand," he embarks with great gentility, "the bartender had to open a new bottle of wine in order to pour—"

"Okay," my father says, dismissing the finer points of the argument with a wave of his hand, "then I tell you what we do. This is what we do. I tell you. You bring us the check for the wine. We pay for the wine. And then we go."

A deft bargaining strategy on my father's behalf.

"Perhaps you would also care to order dinner?" The manager presses his luck.

And in response my father calmly reiterates the game plan: "The check. We pay. We go."

The entire restaurant seems to have fallen silent as the manager and his waitress make their way to the back, where our bill will be tallied. Where will we go now, my father and

I? Where will we find food? There is ponderous silence between us. I wait for an icebreaker but my father says nothing. It's my turn.

"That's really interesting about the seamstresses," I murmur. "About how the seamstresses started the revolution."

"What's that?" My father lifts his head.

"I was just saying that it's really interesting what Trotsky said about the seamstresses starting the revolution and that I want to read *The History of the Russian Revolution*." My voice has grown louder. "Chapter six."

"Yes," my father says with fatigue.

"I was thinking that it's—"

But before I can continue, from out of the swampy darkness the waitress emerges, holding, surprisingly and miraculously, a carafe filled with red wine.

"Zinfandel" is all she says, and pours like a defeated soldier forced to serve the enemy king.

There is contrition on my father's face, and he crosses his hands in front of his belly as if to assure her that despite his victory he has no intention of gloating.

"Look how she fills the glass all the way to the top," he says, thinking this will be seen as some sort of an accomplishment by the waitress. She smiles meekly.

"Some people say the glass is half full," my father presses, "but when it is wine it should always be filled to the top."

She reads the specials in an automatic voice. The dishes have Persian names. I bury my head in the menu, pretending to be considering the full range of options. The foods are unfamiliar. They are unfamiliar because I am my mother's son and my mother is Jewish and the one time she attempted to cook an Iranian meal was a disappointing failure. And we both knew it.

My father listens to the waitress intently. He asks if this dish has eggplant, if the other dish is fried. He orders for both of us. He says thank you a lot, smiles a lot, bats his eyelashes a lot, asks for extra rice and a side of onions—if it's not too much trouble. When she's gone he raises his glass to me. "A toast to your belated birthday."

I raise mine.

"To the young man," he says.

"I'm almost thirty-one, Pop," I say. "I don't feel like a young man."

"That's the contradiction," he says. "I don't feel like an old man."

Clink.

Then my father spills the red wine down his shirt.

I was nine years old the first time I came back to New York City. My mother had packed a bag and put me on an airplane and sent me by myself for the weekend. Why she didn't come with me, I do not know. I had never been on an airplane before, and I had the expectation that I would be able to see the entire earth the way astronauts do. But it was cloudy the entire way, and the only things I could make out from my window were white marshmallow mountains. The flight attendant gave me peanuts and I ate them and then she gave me more. It was my brother who met me at the airport and took me home. He was eighteen now and living with his girlfriend in an apartment a few floors above my father's apartment in Brooklyn. My father was nowhere to be seen the entire weekend. Nor was my sister. Perhaps they were out of town. Perhaps they were at meetings. As for Dianne, she had already been dropped by my father, who had moved on to other women. And a few years later, after an unsuccessful run for governor of New York, Dianne would make the mistake of organizing an event for International Women's Day, be tried for violating Article VIII, Section II of the Socialist Workers Party charter—collaborating with nonmembers without authorization—and be expelled.

It had been three years since I had left New York City, and I no longer recognized it. Everything seemed louder, faster, dirtier than I remembered, and my life from that time felt like it had happened long ago and to someone else. I saw it only as a dream. During the day, my brother and his girlfriend took me to the Botanical Garden, and we walked around and looked at the flowers and they bought me ice cream. I kept thinking I might see my old friend Britton there somehow, some way, but it never happened. My brother talked about the time we had visited the garden with my father and sister and Dianne. "Do you remember that?" he asked. "Do you remember the turtle, Zero, that we buried?" But I didn't remember. That night his girlfriend and he made dinner, and then the three of us lay in bed and watched television for hours, laughing and joking. When *The Incredible Hulk* came on, I jumped up and down on the mattress as if I was the Incredible Hulk and my brother was the bad guy and his girlfriend was the damsel in distress. In our rowdy excitement, my brother accidentally punched his girlfriend in the breast and she squealed in pain. "I'm so sorry!" he cried out, and put his arm around her and cradled her breast. Then the two of them got quiet. When the weekend was over, I didn't want to leave. My brother sat with me on the subway to the airport and I said nothing. He kept trying to make jokes to cheer me up, but I just stared out glumly at the advertisements on the wall. "Look," my brother exclaimed as the subway surfaced from underground, "there's not a cloud in the sky today. You're going to be able to see the entire earth."

It's nearly midnight when we leave the restaurant. My thirtieth birthday dinner is now officially over. I've overeaten as usual, and I feel bloated and heavy.

"Good night, sir," the manager says at the doorway, bowing toward my father and me.

"Good night," my father says, bowing in return. They have let bygones be bygones. My father says something in Persian and the manager smiles and says something back. "Shh," my mother would tell me if we ever approached dark men on the street conversing in a foreign language. And when we had passed she would say to herself, "They were speaking Persian."

Once outside, my father puts the baseball cap back on. *International Brotherhood of Electrical Workers.*

There's a nice mist covering everything, softening the

streets and the buildings. It's quiet. We pass an old-fashioned lamppost.

"That's very nice," my father says with genuine appreciation.

"It's real nice, Pop."

"I think it's gas," he says. "Sidsky, did you know that when I was a little boy in Tabriz we never had gaslights?"

"I didn't know that."

"Tabriz went directly from no light to electric lights. That's the kind of thing that happens in a backward country. The Law of Combined and Uneven Development."

"What's that, Pop?"

"The Law of Combined and Uneven Development," he says again.

"What's it mean?"

"Trotsky writes about it. Two countries—one that exploits and the other that . . . you know. There are things that develOPED unevenly. But combined. Trotsky writes about it . . ." He trails off.

A few cars pass, then someone on a bicycle. My father and I walk in silence. Each in our own thoughts. What are his thoughts? We pass Bryant Park, and in the darkness the trees look like hands. Across the street is my office. I'll be back there tomorrow morning at nine.

And then the subway station looms before us. My father stops and stands in front of me, the splotch of red wine, now dried, running like a birthmark across his chest.

"Sidsky," my father says excitedly, "we should do this again soon."

"Sure," I say.

Then he ponders for a moment, calculating in his head. "Maybe the week after next. Maybe then."

"That sounds good," I say. I know what will happen, of course: Things will come up and the week after next will turn into the month after next, which will turn into six months. I will turn thirty-one. "The week after next sounds good," I say.

"It was nice walking with you, Sidsky."

"It was nice walking with you too."

"Happy birthday, Sidsky."

"Thanks, Pop."

He holds out his hand and we shake like friendly acquaintances.

"Good night," I say.

Then he pulls me to him suddenly, catching me off balance, and he hugs me awkwardly, his stubble brushing against my face. We hold each other tightly for a moment, slightly off center, twisted like metal, his elbow poking into my chest, a vague approximation of an embrace.

"Be good," he whispers in my ear.

The subway is empty except for a few bored souls. I take a seat across from a black man covered in a fine gray dust and wearing construction boots. He watches me closely as I unfold *The Militant*—the first issue of my twelve-week subscription. Two thoughts of equal weight appear in my brain simultaneously. One is that I will be hailed by him for being a liberator who understands his plight and the plight of all those who labor. The other thought is that he is an informant for the government.

I skim some of the articles. The reporting rings familiar and I realize that much of the information has been culled from things I've read in *The New York Times,* rewritten now with a Marxist bent. The words *imperialism* and *capitalism* have been inserted throughout, and Bill Clinton is always referred to as William Clinton so as to eliminate any traces of bourgeois familiarity.

The subway stops, and the black man stands and exits. I watch him walk away. His pants are fraying and he has a slight limp, a hitch in his step that causes him to lean to his left. The doors ding-dong closed and the train pulls out of the station, passing him resting against the railing at the foot of the stairs, summoning his strength before he attempts the ascent. *Socialism will save you.* I look down at *The Militant* and I'm suddenly struck by how much it resembles a high school newspaper. The type seems too big, for one thing, the photos too grainy, and, besides, the entire thing is only sixteen pages thick. You can feel an earnestness behind the effort, a diligence that doesn't quite live up to the size of its ideas. It's a newspaper aspiring to be a newspaper aspiring to world revolution.

There's an article about the latest subscription drive. I study the table that has been provided to show the weekly progress. The goal for the entire United States is listed at 968. That is to say that out of a possible three hundred million people the Socialist Workers Party hopes to sell 968 subscriptions. Out of eight million people in New York City the goal is listed at 120, of which fifteen subscriptions have already been sold. There are five more weeks to go. They will most likely make their goal, of course. They almost always do. There is always the extraordinary distance to reach, the insurmountable odds that can only be overcome by a disciplined, fighting cadre. There are always the articles each week that chronicle how many subscriptions have been sold, how many are still needed to be sold, and what it reflects about the overall class consciousness of workers in the United States. There are the editorials that urge the comrades on to sell and sell. Then there is the blazing headline that heralds a miracle in the eleventh hour. As a little boy I had dreamed of those goals being met. We were always just one more subscription away, one more *Militant,* one more pamphlet, one more book. All we needed was one more and we would win, the revolution would come. Sometimes we made that goal and sometimes we didn't, but no matter, it always resolved itself the same way: In a few weeks there would be another subscription drive, and we would begin again.

I realize I have now become the sixteenth subscription for New York City.

14

MY FATHER DOESN'T KNOW, BUT when I was a little boy my mother hung a black-and-white framed photograph of him over my bed. It had been taken about a year before I was born, and it shows my father standing behind a podium giving a speech to delegates at a political conference somewhere in the Midwest. In the photograph he is wearing a white shirt and a dark tie and a dark wool jacket, and pinned to his jacket is his name tag, and he is balding and slightly unshaven, and he has his glasses on. Covering the front of the podium is a portrait of a man or woman whose face is entirely obscured by a sign that says *Dekalb*. My father is glancing down at his notes as he speaks—looking as calm and self-assured as always.

Eventually I figured out that the hidden face hanging in front of the podium was not that of an Iranian revolutionary, as I had originally assumed, but of Che Guevara. This was an exhilarating revelation for me, because while my father felt like a stranger, Che did not, and so I felt somewhat included. My mother had been sure to inform me on all the major aspects of Che's life: his contribution to the Cuban Revolution; his famous, belligerent speech at the UN; his execution in the jungles of Bolivia. Years of falling asleep and waking beneath the photograph slowly fused the two revolutionaries together for me until Che began to seem so personal that I believed he belonged to me, and that he was my father and my father was Che, and it was now my father in the portrait and Che standing before the podium giving a speech about my father.

What I also learned from my mother was that my parents had considered naming me Che; his execution had taken place the year before I was born. In the end, though, they had opted against it, reasoning that a name like Che Sayrafiezadeh would have presented far too many obstacles for me in my life. I have always found this explanation highly dubious, considering that the alternative my parents finally settled on was certainly not picked with the thought of easing my passage through this world. My father once confided in me that the names of his three children could be viewed as a way to track his political maturity. When he told me this he meant it not as a compliment but as a *supreme* compliment. We were walking through Prospect Park and it had just rained, and there was such an air of confessional intimacy that I could not help but be captivated.

Presumably, my brother was not named Jacob with any political considerations in mind but rather familial ones. There are three Jacobs on my mother's side: Jacob Finkelstein, her grandfather, a landlord; Jacob Klausner, her great-uncle, a florist; and Jacob Epp (née Epstein), the hero in my uncle's novel *Something About a Soldier*. There is a nice symmetry in the first Jacob being from her father's side, the second being from her mother's, and the third being altogether imaginary. That my father—who has no Jacobs on his side—would have conceded the indulgence of naming a child after a florist or a landlord is evidence to me that his personality, his world outlook, his relationship to his wife were once so vastly different as to be virtually unrecognizable. By the time my sister was born three years later, though, my father had begun gravitating toward ideas of revolution, as Jamileh was named after Djamila Bouhired, a member of the Algerian National Liberation Front, who had been imprisoned, tortured, and nearly executed in her struggle against French occupation.

When we arrive at me, five years later, my father returns to matters of ancestry, but this time it's his own ancestry, his uncle Saïd Salmasi, an Iranian revolutionary who has been credited with establishing the first modern school in Iran. In 1907, nearly three decades before my father was born, Saïd Salmasi was killed fighting against the Shah in the failed first Iranian Revolution. What a powerful antidote he must have been to my father's own father, a former businessman who had lost his wealth years earlier. By the time my father was born in 1934, he was impoverished and unemployed. He was also fifty-three years old. And what a powerful antidote Salmasi would have been to my father's mother, who was blind, or nearly blind, and just as helpless as her aging husband. They were apolitical parents. My father has told me so. Powerless and apolitical, content to wait out World War II and the occupation of Iran without protest or complaint. My father, however, has described how as a little seven-year-old boy he would climb a hill after school and watch the long lines of Soviet vehicles rumble below him, ceaseless and disinterested, one after the other, until he became so incensed that he would pick up a handful of pebbles and hurl them at the trucks, *ping ping ping*. Day after day he would enact this ritual, until one day his pebble shattered a windshield and the snaking traffic came to a halt. The little boy was apprehended by the soldiers and taken to the local authorities, who in turn took him home, where he was instructed to sit out the rest of the war with his parents, waiting for others to decide what should happen.

Saïd Salmasi surely would have done something during World War II. And he would have done something that night in 1953 when the Shah's tanks rolled past and all my father could do was go back inside. And he would have done something in 1979 when the revolution he had been killed in seventy years earlier finally returned in full fury.

My father called the night before he moved back to Iran. I was in bed with the lights off when the phone rang. Our phone never rang, and the sound startled me out of the early stages of sleep. Through the bedroom door I could hear my mother answer, and by the voice she was using I knew immediately that it was my father on the other end. It was a confident voice with a touch of breeziness, the kind of voice that one might use at a job interview to impress a potential employer. There was no other time when I heard that voice.

"The workers and peasants of Iran have been struggling for one century," she said with aplomb.

Then my father's response.

"Imperialism's boot," my mother said.

My father's response.

Her response.

I listened to hear mention of me, of my recent tenth birthday, but there was no mention. Nor was there mention of my brother and sister. The two would fend for themselves. They were still teenagers, but they were solid, upstanding members of the party. Future leaders. They had no real need for a father anymore.

And then they wound it up, my parents. My mother said good-bye. There was something good-natured in her good-bye. It wasn't a good-bye that implied permanent separation; it was a so-long-see-you-around-sometime good-bye. Then she hung up the phone. *Click.*

And then she sobbed. Great sobs. Shakespearean. Her wails shook our tiny apartment and the other tiny apartments in our building. They shook me in my bed, lying there in the darkness, pretending to be asleep.

When morning came, I played dumb when she broke the news to me. Neither of our faces betrayed a thing. It was January and a deep chill had descended over Pittsburgh, but after breakfast I went outside anyway. I tossed a tennis ball against the brick wall in the backyard, imagining that it was summertime, that I was Reggie Jackson throwing the ball, and that the wall was Reggie Jackson hitting the ball. The green ball would bounce high into the air and then come down hard, roll and stop. In my mind, each hit was the hit that won the game.

It made no difference, of course, in my mother's and my day-to-day life if my father lived in the United States or Iran. In the same way it made no difference to my brother and sister what became of their mother. My parents had succeeded in building an insurmountable wall between the two factions of the family, and one can only imagine the calisthenics it takes to avoid fellow members of a small organization founded on the idea of universal brotherhood.

After my father's departure, my mother took to removing the telephone from its hook each night. This was her way of declaring "You are still my husband, but you are never coming back. I know that now. And I honor it by taking the phone off the hook. We are now, both sides, unreachable." The phone could not be unplugged from the wall, or the ringer turned off, so after she had kissed me good night she would simply set the receiver on the floor. In the dark, the dial tone cried out as if it were a strange animal, its long, steady beep filling up the quiet apartment. I would listen to it and stare off into the black. After a good amount of time had passed, a male voice would appear, pleasant but urgent, like a messenger bringing news that could potentially be troubling.

"There appears to be a receiver off the hook. If you'd like to place a call, please hang up and try your call again."

There was something embarrassing about this recorded voice assuming that the receiver could have only been displaced by oversight. *I only need to make you aware of such an oversight and the situation will of course be immediately remedied.* Three times the man would repeat this—"There appears to be a receiver off the hook . . ."—and three times my mother would ignore him. After his third try he would give up and let a shrill, high-pitched beep take his place. Despite knowing the pattern, I was always shocked by the sound, incessant and slightly chemical, as if alerting us to a fire. My heart pounded along with its rhythm. Fire. Fire. Fire. On and on it went, threatening to continue unabated until the morning. Had my mother developed some type of immunity and now I was the only one who could hear it?

Then the sound would stop abruptly, so abruptly that it continued roaming through my head. Eventually silence would drift in, take over, permanent silence. It was as if the phone had exhausted itself trying to get placed back on the hook.

My mother and I were on our own. We were floating on a raft in the ocean. It was night, and the waves were gently rocking us up and down and from side to side, and all we could do was hope that the raft would not spring a leak or water spill over the edge. There was no one anywhere in the world who could save us now. The black silence covered us, a silence so encompassing that I found myself desiring the return of the phone's harsh, grating cry. Then I would drift off to sleep with Che hovering above me.

15

I RUN INTO KAREN IN front of the public library on Fifth Avenue. She has gone there on her lunch break to check out a book called *Do What You Love, The Money Will Follow: Discovering Your Right Livelihood.* There are giant rainbow stripes on the cover. We stand on the street for a while as she tells me about how she's wanted to be an artist since she was a little girl and her father would take her to buy supplies at the art store on weekends. When it was time for college, though, her parents thought she should have a more "practical" education, so instead of going to the School of Visual Arts in Manhattan, she ended up studying at a liberal arts college in Connecticut, where she balanced a major in art with a minor in marketing.

"Now look at me," she says. "I'm a project manager for Martha Stewart."

I tell her I know how she feels because I'm also hoping to one day do what I love and have the money follow. And then, since we happen to be standing in front of the library, I describe how when I was a little boy my mother would send me in to return overdue books without paying the fine.

She laughs. Then she stops. "That's a weird story," she says.

Each morning while I'm riding my bicycle to the office I tell myself that today's the day I'm going to ask Karen out. And each evening while I'm riding home I bemoan my lack of nerve. Sometimes I reason with myself that most likely she'll say no anyway and all I'll end up achieving is a permanently awkward work environment for the two of us. But the next day we'll have a fun, friendly chat about something like how to find a good apartment in New York City and before we know it an hour's passed. Or I'll happen to turn around in my chair to get something and I'll catch her staring at me. When our eyes meet she'll smile and look away. *Ask her now!* But I don't. I can't. And once again on the way home I'll berate myself.

In seventh grade there was a pretty girl in my class who I would often find watching me when I looked up from my desk. I enjoyed her stare but I was also confused by it. I did not believe that she found me handsome, that anyone found me handsome. And after a month of her smiling and blushing and getting no response whatsoever, she turned her attention to a good-looking boy in our class. Which made sense to me.

This morning it is not just Karen's presence at the edge of my desk that's causing me my usual turmoil but also what she's chosen to talk about: a strike at the Museum of Modern Art, where she once worked. Last night, she tells me, she went to stand with former coworkers on a picket line in front of the museum, where she screamed at the top of her lungs, "Modern art! Ancient wages!" And also, "Lowry, Lowry, what's your salary?" Referring to Glenn Lowry, director of the museum, whose salary is, of course, immeasurably higher than the secretaries', librarians', and cafeteria workers' who have been on strike for three months now.

"I never get to scream," she says, laughing. "It was cathartic."

I'm not able to share in her good humor. As she talks, my mind races to come up with something to say that will lead her from her experience last night to a greater understanding of socialism. Or something to that effect. I'm not sure what. There's always something, though, to be said, something to be done, something to nudge the masses into consciousness. *The Militant* was always phrasing things like *we argued,* or *we explained,* or *we discussed* when describing conversations with workers. And by the end of the article the workers always bought an issue. Or a subscription.

"It's good you went," I say. "It's an important thing to do." I can hear the patronizing sound in my voice, but I'm powerless to stop it. All I can hope is that she doesn't notice. There's a smile plastered on my face, trying to hide my condescension, which in turn is trying to hide my ignorance. It's my ignorance that feels the most troubling. I've never stood on a picket line in my life. Nor do I want to. Yet I feel like I should have some authority over Karen on this matter. I once got into a shouting match with a girlfriend over the Soviet occupation of Poland during World War II, even though I knew nothing about it and my girlfriend was Polish.

"Don't go in there!" Karen says she screamed at the patrons about to enter the museum. "Don't fucking go in there!" As if it were a haunted house they stood before. Some went in regardless, but many turned away. And when they did, everyone cheered.

"Are the workers planning to link up with other struggles?" I ask.

She doesn't know.

"Did it have an international tone?"

"A what?"

Words rush into my throat, trying to get out all at once. Words like *working class, ruling class, dictatorship of the proletariat.* I feel choked by them. I want to change the subject. *The subject must not be changed!* I want to crawl under the desk.

"The union organizer gave me a whistle," she says, but before she can continue with her amusing anecdote I cut her off.

"I should probably get back to work."

She's startled. "Oh."

I am full of relief when she leaves. Then full of regret. What does she think of me now? The words in my throat recede, and I am left remembering how I'd watch my mother on those Saturday mornings as she "discussed" that week's topic with a passerby until my mother grew frustrated and would nod and smile, as if to say "I'm sorry you're such a fool," and walk away. "Some workers cannot be won over," she'd tell me.

It's noon and I'm hungry. A few blocks away is a Caribbean restaurant and the thought of going there to eat something good makes me happy. On my way out, I pass Karen standing front of the copy machine. Her back is to me and she's holding a giant stack of magazines.

"I'm going to get some lunch at the Caribbean restaurant," I say.

"That sounds tasty," she says, without turning around. "See you later."

"I'll finish everything up when I get back."

"Okay," she says.

"I won't be long."

"Okay."

"Do you want to come with me?"

She turns and looks at me. The machine whirrs and whirrs.

"Do you want to come with me to the Caribbean restaurant to get some lunch?"

"Yes," she says. "I'd love to."

16

ACCORDING TO *The Militant,* THE very first thing my father and a dozen other Iranian exiles did when their plane touched down at Mehrabad Airport in Tehran on the afternoon of January 22, 1979, was to catch a taxi to a news conference at the Intercontinental Hotel, where they announced the official formation of *Hezb-e Kargaran-e Sosialist* (the Socialist Workers Party). It had been twenty-five years since my father left Iran for the University of Minnesota. The likelihood that the Shah's secret police, SAVAK, would have tossed him in a torture chamber the moment he stepped from the plane had prevented him from returning for even a visit. Now, though, SAVAK's agents were being hunted, millions were marching through the streets, and the Shah had packed his suitcases to go on an "extended vacation."

"Dear comrades," Jack Barnes wrote in greeting, "the formation of the *Hezb-e Kargaran-e Sosialist*—the first Trotskyist party on Iranian soil—is an historic and inspiring event. . . . You have taken a major step in building a mass revolutionary party based on the principles of Lenin and Trotsky. Only such a party can lead the fight for a socialist Iran to a successful conclusion. Long live the Iranian revolution! Long live *Hezb-e Kargaran-e Sosialist.*"

My father and his comrades wasted no time. One of their first acts was to go against the wishes of Khomeini—who was just about to arrive from his exile in Paris—and call for the democratic election of a constituent assembly by secret ballot. They also began publication of a fortnightly newspaper called *Kargar* (the *Worker*). In addition, they printed and distributed thousands of copies of a fourteen-point *Bill of Rights for Workers and Toilers of Iran,* which included the demand for a forty-hour workweek, the abolition of business secrets, full rights and equality for women ("this great mass of humanity"), and the confiscation of land from big landowners without any compensation.

"Capitalists," the second point reads, "property owners, landlords, the bosses of the big companies . . . have maintained total secrecy. All the books and accounts of the secret transactions of these rich must be opened so that their robberies will be known to everyone."

In the face of such excitement and enthusiasm, there could be no cessation in my mother's commitment. On Friday and Sunday evenings she continued to attend her meetings, seemingly unfazed that many of those meetings were now about Iran. And on Saturday mornings she rose at dawn and went off to sell *The Militant,* even though within its pages were not only articles extolling the efforts of her husband but photographs of him as well, handsome and smiling in a suit and tie.

What had first looked like a clean and final break with my father had become a deeper engagement. In the morning he appeared at our breakfast table while my mother and I listened to National Public Radio. "Shh," she would say to me when the American correspondent in Tehran had been introduced. I was not astute enough to be able to discern what was good news from what was bad news and had to rely on the expression of my mother's face for clues. I would watch her intently as she watched the radio intently, her head cocked like she was listening for footsteps in the hallway.

The news was chaotic, uncertain, above all portentous. There was talk of closing American embassies; of the rise of Khomeini; of the chance of an oil embargo; of U.S. troops being trained for possible deployment.

"There are dark clouds on the horizon," National Security Adviser Zbigniew Brzezinski told us.

"What about the *shoras* that are being formed all over the country?" my mother would ask, referring to the workers' councils that were being likened by *The Militant* to the soviets of the Russian Revolution. "Are those the dark clouds you're afraid of?"

But her question would go unanswered, and soon the radio would switch to another topic, a happier one. As it did, my father receded and the two of us who remained at the table would go about the business of eating breakfast.

In the evening, after we had finished our dinner and the dishes had been cleared away, we would sit together and watch Walter Cronkite on the *CBS Evening News* as he informed us of all that had transpired that day in Iran. Cronkite's voice, authoritative and genial—the voice of a grandfather—would be juxtaposed unkindly against the images of violence and tumult, tanks in the street, dark men with dark beards inton-ing in a foreign language. My father was somewhere among those men.

"What about twenty-five years of U.S. imperialism?" my mother would ask. "You don't want to talk about that, do you?"

"And that's the way it is," Cronkite would respond, closing as he always did with his trademark line. "Monday, February twelfth, 1979." Then my mother would switch the television off. After which I would sit at my desk in my bedroom and finish my homework and then get into bed. My mother lean-ing above me to kiss me on the forehead, wishing me sweet dreams, turning off the light, and closing the bedroom door. In the darkness, I would wait to hear that man's familiar voice filling the apartment. "There appears to be a receiver off the hook. If you'd like to make a call . . ."

My father's presence in our lives did not limit itself solely to current events but found other ways to make its appearance.

"You know, your eyes are like his," my mother said to me one day.

In the bathroom mirror I looked at my eyes. They were brown eyes. My mother had brown eyes. Why were my eyes not my mother's eyes? I had always assumed the only inheritance I had received from my father were my unpro-nounceable first and last names. All else I had conceded to my brother and sister long ago.

A week passed.

"You know, your hair is like his," she said.

"It is?"

"Brown wavy hair."

And sometime later, standing in the kitchen: "Your hands are like his. Just like that. Just the way you're holding that glass like that."

"Your eyebrows are like his."

"Your eyelashes are like his."

Did everything belong to my father? Yes, my mother was saying, yes. Take it all. You don't want to be left looking like me. I am ugly, but he is handsome.

"Your teeth are like his. He had strong white teeth. He could crack walnuts with his teeth."

"Your fingernails are like his."

And once, inexplicably, uttered as if it were a dream and I was walking through thick dream smoke: "Do you have a brown ring around your penis like he had?"

"I don't know," I said. "No, I don't think so," I said.

17

I HAD NO FRIENDS IN my neighborhood. We had moved so many times that I had lost the ability to breach that childhood wall of shyness. Even two years after our arrival in what was to be the final neighborhood my mother and I lived in together, I still felt like a newcomer. It was a pretty neighborhood too, much prettier than any we had lived in before, with trees and yards, an indication that my mother had either gotten a raise or had simply grown exhausted from such unremitting bleakness. Or both.

Just around the corner from my apartment building was a wide concrete playground, one block wide, that I had always—always in passing—seen filled with boys my age. It was part jungle gym, part basketball court, part baseball field, all encircled by a tall chain-link fence that in the summertime became overgrown with ivy.

"Why don't you go out and play with the boys in the playground," my mother would encourage. "It's such a nice day today." But I would never go.

The only friends I had were from the elementary school I attended, and that was miles away. My mother had applied to this school when we first moved to Pittsburgh because it was considered a fine school and a paradigm of integration. Located on the eastern edge of the city, in the middle of a poor black community, it would have been almost entirely black if not for the busing in of white children from more distant, more wealthy neighborhoods. I was white and so I had been accepted.

In the beginning, the bus ride had been torturous for me. A swirly, whirly, hour-long affair that had caused me to vomit on several occasions and be kept in the nurse's office. There was some irony in the fact that the first demonstration I ever recall attending was in support of desegregation busing. It had taken place in Boston just a few weeks after a thousand white people had surrounded a high school there, chanting "Lynch the niggers." We had driven up from New York City with comrades, arriving in what felt like the dead of night. It was also the dead of winter, and I wasn't dressed warm enough. Midway through the march, my mother had no choice but to leave me inside the cab of a truck as she continued onward. I have a single image of sitting next to a strange comrade as I stared down at my blistering five-year-old feet, unable to draw a correlation between the cold weather and the pain in my shoes.

In Pittsburgh I lived farther from my school than any of the other students and so was always the first one picked up in the morning and the last one dropped off in the afternoon. It was hard for me to disregard the fact that just half a block away from my apartment was an elementary school that I could have walked to in about thirty seconds. I was even on the school bus before the bus monitor got on, a chubby, cheery black woman—the only black person on the bus—who had freckles and whom I had once tried to have vote for the Socialist Workers Party candidate for mayor. "Oh, sweetie," she had said, "he's not going to win." There were always at least fifteen minutes where it was just the bus driver and me riding along in bored silence as we slowly passed out of my unfamiliar neighborhood or slowly back into my unfamiliar neighborhood. I would spend the time staring absently at the driver's hands as he spun the enormous steering wheel like he was navigating a boat over the ocean.

The first children to be picked up after me were a brother and sister whom I despised. It had something to do with the fact that they looked even more poor and uncared for than I, especially the little girl, who was my age and whose knees and elbows always seemed to be dirty. She had blond hair and wore thick eyeglasses, and other children—myself included—would tease her with no apparent impact. Rather than being despondent or humiliated, she affected a pompous, superior attitude toward us. Once, I cornered her at school when the teacher was nowhere to be seen and stood in a row with other boys as we took turns punching her as hard as we could in the arm. This, too, did not seem to faze her. Later, when she reported what I had done, I denied all, affecting my own pompous, superior attitude, which was good enough to convince the teacher that it was the little girl who was lying.

Soon, more prosperous children would board the bus and it would quickly fill with the sounds of chatter and laughter, which I would happily join. Often I would crouch behind the seats with other boys and play a game called "pencil fighting," where two players took turns using their pencil to try to snap their opponent's pencil in half. The game was immensely popular but it was against the rules to play, both in school and on the bus. There was a rumor that someone had once lost an eye from a flying pencil shard. Generally we played with thin, brown, anemic Pittsburgh Public School pencils that had no eraser. We had gotten the pencils for free and therefore risked nothing.

The school had been built just a few years earlier, and it radiated a sense of grandeur and opulence. The floors were carpeted, the classrooms spacious, and everything was clean, brightly lit, and perfectly in its place. I believed that everyone who attended this school was wealthy. Even the black children whom my mother told me were poor seemed wealthy. My friend Jesse was black and had no father and lived in the housing project around the corner, but his clothes were always new and his mother owned a car and his apartment building looked nice from the bus window. "It only looks nice from the outside," my mother said. Even so, I could not bring myself to pity him. I thought he was the most handsome of all my classmates, with smooth dark skin and broad shoulders. He was also the strongest. When we were in third grade I had watched him lift a bullying older boy off his feet and throw him to the ground. He was a master at both pencil fighting and dodgeball, and at lunch he would open up his packet of plastic silverware by slamming it on the cafeteria table so that the knife sliced clean through the top. I admired him to such a degree that once during free time he had persuaded me to help pick up scraps of paper off the classroom floor. Together we had crawled on our hands and knees under and around the desks until it became apparent that the purpose of this was not to clean the room but to look up the girls' skirts. A service to the community had become a violation to the community. Nevertheless, it fascinated me that he was interested only in the black girls' panties, while I was interested in both, even those of the girl I had punched. When the time came to sit in a circle and read aloud, I could make eye contact with no one.

He had come to visit me only once. A Saturday afternoon that had been made possible because his mother was will-ing to drive him. We spent the day playing football in my backyard, and he won every game. Then we played baseball with a tennis ball, and he hit the ball on the roof. For lunch my mother served us tangerines and cheese sandwiches. Jesse consumed great quantities and asked for more. I feared she would refuse him. She asked him questions about school and his favorite classes and what he wanted to be when he grew up. "A football player," he said. Afterward we went into my bedroom, closed the door, selected two pencils from my desk, and pencil-fought.

That evening, when his mother came to take him home, she stood by the front door of the apartment but did not come in. She was wearing slacks and had long hair. There was glamour about her.

"Did you boys have fun?" she asked.

"Yes," we said.

I watched as she stood there awkwardly in the doorway, taking in her surroundings. I saw what she saw: my mother smiling, with short graying hair and baggy pants; socks dangling over the arm of a chair; the bed/couch piled with papers; the unfortunate closet door, flung wide open, with a million *Militant*s running all the way to the edge. I was prepared for her to exclaim *"What* are *those?"* At her feet, as if it had floated like a leaf and happened to land there, was the latest issue. She looked down. WHY WORKERS NEED A LABOR PARTY NOW.

"Did you boys clean up?" she asked us.

There could be no disputing that my white friends from school were wealthy. Tab's father was a doctor who had once paid a visit to class to talk to us about how to grow up to be a doctor. I didn't know what his mother did for a living, but she was always at home when I went over to play. In order to get to his house I had to ride on a different school bus, which went through different neighborhoods. I would usually go after school on a Friday with my toothbrush and a small bag of clothes so that I could spend the night. His house was not nearly as large or resplendent as my uncle's, but I thought it was spectacular nonetheless. Rooms opened onto other rooms that opened onto a deck that overlooked the backyard. Dinner might be chicken and mashed potatoes and gravy and a bowl of ice cream. I would eat from a plate that matched the other plates, sitting in a chair that matched the table. "And how was school today, boys?" his father-doctor would ask. In the basement was an air hockey table that we had once tiptoed down from his bedroom to play in the middle of the night. The cool air of the table had blown up into my face as we slammed the plastic puck back and forth, back and forth. "Get back to bed!" his father had shouted.

Tab had befriended me when I first arrived from New York City in the middle of my second-grade year. This despite the fact that I had spent a whole month inquiring cleverly, "How much do I owe you, Tab?" He had a rectangular-shaped head and moles on his face and had read, or was in the process of reading, every *Hardy Boys* book ever written. Because of this I considered him supremely intelligent.

The first time Tab ever visited me in my new neighborhood, I was violently aware that the bus ride I had grown so inured to was relentlessly long. Even as we played and joked with the other children, I feared that he would at any moment stand and demand to go no further. Upon arrival at my apartment building I had played a clever joke where I walked right past the building as if my house were farther up the street. "Just kidding," I said. Once through the front door, I was immediately overcome with that same despondent feeling I would get after visiting my uncle. Except now a witness had come along with me. I saw how obviously unkempt the foyer was and the way the mailboxes had all been broken so that the doors hung loosely from their hinges. Names of previous tenants had been written directly on the metal and then scratched off and replaced with new names that had then been scratched off and replaced. On and on. My mother, however, had placed a clean white label across our mailbox that clearly read *Apt. 4 Harris/Sayrafiezadeh,* as if roommates resided there, or an unmarried couple, or a married couple who had decided to keep their names.

I led Tab up the two flights of stairs to the apartment and unlocked the door. We had arrived an hour and a half before my mother would be home from work, and the place thrummed with silence. "You have to take your shoes off," I said, and even this embarrassed me: a proscription before he had entered. I was aware of how small the apartment was, how fragile, like the floor might break if we both stepped at the same time. When he asked for the bathroom, I played another joke by telling him to go through my bedroom, down the hall, and up the stairs. Of course there was no hall and there were no stairs. "Just kidding." In the kitchen I served him a plate of graham crackers and a glass of milk. When he had finished, I gave him more without asking so as to display some sense of abundance.

At dinner, I grew angry when I saw the unexceptional meal my mother had prepared. Peas, carrots, rice, an acorn squash. My mother had sprinkled the squash with brown sugar, and so I knew she saw it as a special treat. Tab ate only the brown sugar. "You're supposed to eat the rest," my mother said. Tab didn't understand. She showed him, bending over his shoulder and scooping the yellow flesh away. "See," she said, "look at all of that."

We talked about school and our favorite classes and what we wanted to be when we grew up.

"I want to be an actor," I said.

"I want to be a detective," Tab said.

"I see," my mother said. She didn't approve.

For dessert she served us each a bowl of Jell-O.

"Do you have whipped cream?" he asked.

No.

I was relieved when dinner was over and we could go to my room and shut the door. On the floor we played a game of Scrabble. Halfway through, my mother opened the door and walked by on her way to the bathroom. She stopped and examined the board with interest.

"What good words!" she said happily. Then she went into the bathroom, where we could hear the tinkle of pee, the flush of the toilet, the running of the faucet.

I didn't know what my friend Victor's parents did for a living, but his house was just as big as Tab's. In fact, he lived not too far from it. He was a tall boy, with brown bushy hair that was always falling in front of his eyes, like a sheepdog. When he spoke, saliva would sometimes gather in the corners of his mouth, so that if he was not wiping the hair out of his face, he was wiping the saliva from his lips. One day after school his mother had shown us how to make "pies" using paper plates and his father's shaving cream, which we then carried out into the backyard to smash each other in the face with. This was spectacular, unheard-of lawlessness, and I held his mother in high esteem because of it. For his tenth birthday we had gone roller-skating with a group of his friends. At the entrance to the rink, Victor's father had handed him a twenty-dollar bill and said he'd be back in two hours. "I want to see some change from that twenty," he told Victor. We spent the day eating pizza and playing video games until there was less than two dollars left and we had to stop.

I was, of course, beset by my chronic uneasiness and anxiety whenever Victor visited me in my apartment. And it just so happened that one Sunday afternoon, while eating our way through boring cheese sandwiches with my mother, Victor looked up at the bulletin board above the kitchen table and asked, "Who's that?"

The bulletin board was thumbtacked full, as it always was, with the latest clippings and flyers that announced the next meeting and the next demonstration. For many years, though, a *New York Times* clipping of Castro had remained a permanent feature, his beard bushy, his military uniform crisp, his finger jabbing at the air. I observed the image yellowing with time, curling in on itself, as a hundred meals were eaten beneath it, and then a thousand. It was at Castro that Victor pointed.

"That's Fidel Castro," my mother said.

"Who's that?" Victor asked.

"He's the leader of Cuba."

"Why do you have a picture of him?"

"He's a revolutionary."

"What'd he do?"

"He fought for communism."

"Communism's bad."

"No, it's not."

"Yes, it is."

"Capitalism is what's bad."

"I like capitalism."

"Capitalism makes people poor."

"No, it doesn't. It makes people rich."

"That's what they want you to think."

"Who wants me to think that?"

On it went. Neither would relent. My mother took on a patient, patronizing tone that I recognized. "And how do bosses make their money?" she asked Victor, as if she had all day to lead him to the truth. "And what about the workers' right to organize?" Inside, I knew she was seething. Filled with disappointment not just with Victor but with me for the poor judgment to have chosen a friend like Victor. "Are his parents right-wingers?" she would later ask.

And Victor smiled like the whole thing was amusing, like he couldn't believe he had actually found someone who thought communism was good. It was only because he kept using the corner of his shirtsleeve to obsessively push together a small pile of crumbs from his cheese sandwich that I understood he was nervous. And my mother, finding this unsanitary and annoying, kept asking him to stop. But no sooner would Victor stop than he would begin again, so that the debate over communism and capitalism was continually being interrupted by my mother's admonishing voice saying "Please, Victor. Please don't push the crumbs with your sleeve."

———

Not long after that, I caught the school bus home with Victor to spend the night. His parents were having company, so when it was time for dinner, the table was lively with adult talk. A large plate of chicken and mashed potatoes was placed before me and I dug in. "How was school today?" his mother asked us. "What did you read?" "What did the teacher say?" In the middle of making my way through my food, I looked up to see Victor's father staring at me inquisitively, and without any sort of warning he asked: "So, Saïd, what do you think about what's going on over there in Iran?"

The table fell silent. I put my fork down and then picked it back up. It was the first time I had ever been in the presence of someone outside of the Socialist Workers Party who had mentioned Iran. The question had been asked with genuine curiosity, but I disbelieved that curiosity. I was sure there was buried meaning in the inelegant phrase *over there*. I quickly chewed and swallowed what was in my mouth, and then, without thinking, I said loudly to everyone at the table, like I was a man standing behind a podium: "I SUPPORT THE STRUGGLE OF THE IRANIAN WORKERS AND PEASANTS AGAINST U.S. IMPERIALISM."

The words came out like a rush, reflexive and unedited. I was proud of my words. And then I was mortified. What did I just say? There was an awkward interlude where Victor's father looked at me curiously from across the expanse of the table, a smile at his lips. The guests looked at me with interest. As did Victor. A brief image flitted past my eyes where I was standing up from my chair and running from the house. That was followed by an image of me smashing my plate on the floor.

I waited for Victor's father to rejoin, but he said simply, "Well, I just hope those folks over there can work it out."

18

I GRADUATED FROM ELEMENTARY SCHOOL that year. For the commencement ceremony I wore a turtleneck sweater and corduroy pants that my mother had bought the week before from Sears. Everyone else was dressed in a suit. "Where's your suit?" a black boy named Robert asked me. "I didn't feel like wearing it today," I said. In the gymnasium we all sang "Somewhere Over the Rainbow." I sang at the top of my lungs and with great feeling, imagining myself an actor onstage being admired by the audience.

"I have something for you," my mother said to me one morning that summer as she was preparing to leave for work. I was lying in the middle of the living-room floor, obsessing over alphabetizing my stamp collection, and I looked up just in time to see my mother unzip her knapsack and withdraw a small white envelope.

"Here you are," she said.

The envelope was for me but it was unaddressed. It had apparently been passed from my sister onto comrades traveling from New York City to Pittsburgh, who had passed it along to my mother at last night's meeting, who was now passing it along to me. Even before I knew its contents, the envelope had already grown heavy with the acquired weight of legend. I took it carefully and with both hands.

"I'll be home by five-thirty," my mother said, and she shut the front door behind her.

I went into the bedroom and sat down on the edge of my bed. The envelope was already open. Had the contents been read by someone in transit? Inside was a piece of notebook paper, which I removed and unfolded. The paper had been torn cleanly, precisely in half, and on it, written in green ink in an odd mix of both cursive and print, and flaunting the ruled lines, was a letter from my father dated one month earlier, July 23, with the year omitted.

Dear Saïd. He began by saying a comrade had told him I had sold the most number of *Militants* in one demonstration. He said that it had been exciting to hear that. He also said he had received letters and photographs from Martha and that he was proud of me and hoped that I didn't believe what I heard on television about Iran. Iran was in the midst of a revolution, and in fact I had been named after my great-uncle who had fought and died in the first revolution seventy years earlier. Young people were now going around the country teaching other young people how to read and write, because the Shah had never built any schools for them. And then he ended by saying that he hoped my summer was good and that he'd like to hear about it.

When I was done reading, I carefully refolded the piece of paper and put it back inside the envelope. Then I put the envelope in my dresser drawer under a pile of socks. After that I walked back into the living room and was about to sit down with my stamp collection when I was interrupted by the thought that my mother was expecting to have the envelope returned to her. So I went back to the bedroom, retrieved it from my dresser drawer, and then returned to the living room, where I placed it on the edge of her bed. The sun was pouring in through the windows, and I was reminded that it was summertime and that I was inside when I really should be outside. I put on my shoes and went out into the heat, determined to do something. Two blocks away was a shopping district, lined on both sides with restaurants and boutiques, and I strolled the length of the street with the shoppers, pretending that I was also a shopper, stopping here and there to peer into the various window displays of belts and ties glowing with vibrant color, as if they were things that could be eaten. Men and women with shopping bags passed me on both sides, and I heard my mother's voice inside my head saying Look at them, the rich asses. I felt the urge to steal something, but when I reached the end of the street I turned and walked down a different street, this one fronted with modest two-story homes. The sun was at the top of its arc and the pavement had become so hot that my shoes felt as if they were sinking into it, sticking like a fly's feet in chewing gum. Soon I came to a bridge that signified for me a boundary of sorts, and I turned back the way I had come. In the playground by my apartment, I saw a group of boys my age playing football. "Throw it to me, Eric!" "Throw it to me, Michael!" I watched them as they threw it back and forth, and I thought of approaching them, of joining them, but the thought took the place of action.

Back home I reclaimed the envelope, taking it with me into the bedroom and shutting the door, even though there was nothing to shut the door against. I removed the slip of paper and unfolded it again. *Dear Saïd* . . .

I had never received anything from my father, and to receive now a letter written in a tone so casual, so familiar—composed as if it were not the very first letter but one in a series of letters—confused me. There was also an underlying cheeriness in it that seemed to contradict what I thought I knew. I was embarrassed by my confusion. The confusion in turn stoked my embarrassment. And then I was embarrassed by my embarrassment. Add to this my utter disappointment that I could not claim the honor of having sold the most number of *Militant*s in one demonstration. That accomplishment most likely belonged to my brother or sister, who must have been mistaken for me. This made me think that the letter had been composed under a false premise, and I was troubled by a feeling of fraudulence. Not only had I not sold the most number of *Militant*s in one demonstration, I had never sold any *Militant*s at any demonstration. I was too young to sell them, but I knew I should be selling them. I *wanted* to sell them. My only financial contribution was to have once stood on a street corner in the middle of a demonstration in Washington, D.C., with a sandwich board around my neck stuck full of buttons reading *Stop Police Brutality. Vote Socialist Workers,* going for twenty to fifty cents each. I can remember the magnificent sensation of an enormous pot of coins inside my pocket, tilting me to one side and jangling conspicuously with each step. "Money for the revolution," the comrade said to me when I relinquished them at the end of the day, each and every one.

I was further spun by the surprising revelation that all along my mother had been sending my father news of my life. It had been done unbeknownst to me, undertaken perhaps while I was asleep. If it had ever occurred to my mother that I should participate in communicating with my father about myself, she had never said so. Whatever elements of my life she decided to share, I am sure they were chosen so the portrait that emerged was one where all was well and the future was bright. *Here's Saïd on his bicycle. Here's Saïd in the park. Saïd is getting tall.* When she was done gathering the bits and pieces, she swept them into an envelope and sent them off to Iran. And shortly afterward, my father opened the envelope and from those same bits and pieces set about putting together his own portrait of his son, also one that showed all was well and the future was bright. This is why I had the sensation that I was reading a letter written for someone else, a someone else who vaguely resembled me but was not me.

I determined to become that boy in the letter, and I took out a piece of notebook paper and set about composing a response. In my head I invented a story that would regale my father with adventures from my summer. *Today I did . . . ! Yesterday I did . . . !* For many minutes I stared at the blank page, thinking about what I might say and the way I might say it. As I sorted through the details of my life, hoping to find a place to launch, I could feel the assumed identity of that confident boy seeping away from me, being replaced by the boy I was. I saw myself penning the words *I sold the most number of* Militant*s in one demonstration,* but I could not bring myself to lie. Finally I decided that I would begin by simply telling him that in a few weeks I would be entering sixth grade at a new school. But when I lifted the pen and wrote the word *Dear,* I saw that I was facing a grave and perilous obstacle: I had no idea to whom I should address the letter. All the many possibilities seemed to mock me. *Dear Dad. Dear Daddy. Pa. Papa. Poppa. Poppy. Pop.*

The salutation revealed the facade. *Dear Mahmoud Sayrafiezadeh.*

My father had encountered this quandary as well but had encountered it at the end of the letter rather than at the beginning. He had resolved the problem by eluding it, closing his letter by writing the word *Love* and then beneath it—in a rapid, indecipherable hand, squiggling and wiggling and disappearing into illegibility—the only illegible word of the letter: *M~~.*He must have begun to write his first name and, realizing how absurd it was, had decided to cut his losses. *Love, M~~.* It was a signature that landed nowhere. Anyone, anywhere. A ghost.

I never responded to my father, and despite the promising tone of his letter, a tone that looked forward with optimism, I never received another one from him either. Nor did I return the letter to my mother as I had intended but kept it with me, buried deep within my sock drawer.

19

My years of school buses were over. Not a moment too soon. My mother went with me the first time as practice. It was Sunday and it was sunny. We walked out of our apartment building, up the block, and turned left.

"That's all you have to do," she said. "You just turn left and keep walking."

"What if I get lost?"

"You won't get lost."

There was a little grocery store on the corner, and a man in an apron was putting apples in the window. After that it was just houses. Houses and yards. Someone was grilling somewhere. I could smell the smoke. Everything was very quiet, very tranquil. We passed a church with people in suits gathered in front, talking and hugging. Then we turned a corner and came face to face with a steel fence. Standing behind the steel fence was a giant brown-and-white building, windowless, modern, encircled by trees. The trees cast long shadows. A parking lot stood empty.

"There it is," my mother said.

I squeezed through the fence with ease and stood with my hands in my pockets.

———

Aside from the fact that my new school was four times the size, it was similar in many ways to my old school. It was new, it was carpeted, and the student body was almost entirely black. Once again each morning school buses filled with white children would pull in front, and once again each afternoon they would drive away. The school had been named in honor of Florence Reizenstein, a Jewish civil rights activist from Pittsburgh who had fought for the integration of public schools. But the first thing we did my sixth-grade year was take a series of reading and math comprehension tests, one after the other, lasting for several weeks, mind-numbing in their detail. This, it was explained to us, would determine our academic aptitude. When the exams were finally completed and the thousands of answers tallied, the results clearly fell along racial lines, with the majority of the black children being ushered into what were referred to benignly as the "regular" classes. While everyone else, most of whom were white, found themselves at the beginning of October sitting in a classroom that was labeled "scholars."

The separation was absolute. Even the few times that the black and white students came together—lunch, gym, occupational/vocational training—they barely interacted. The school was lavish, with television sets in each classroom and a swimming pool, but I did not feel that the black students benefited from such lavishness. They seemed to be constantly at odds with teachers, who were reproaching them for poor grades and poor behavior. From time to time I would see a black boy or girl I had known from elementary school and they seemed strange to me now, distant, like I was viewing them from afar. Fear and resentment gripped many of the white students, and they would tell stories in private, possibly apocryphal, about someone who had known someone who had strayed into a deserted part of the school, where they had been cornered and beaten by black children. And there were whispered warnings about avoiding the swimming pool, which was said to have been made "greasy."

I was considered a scholar. And I was an excellent student. Attentive, respectful, engaging. For instance, when the science teacher gave us an assignment to construct a periodic table, I went above and beyond what was required and, with assistance from my mother, attached a penny for copper and a nickel for nickel—bested only by the boy who had used a plastic banana for potassium. I became friends almost immediately with a classmate named Daniel. And Daniel became friends with Tab. And the three of us would sit together in class and in the lunchroom, eating amid the spectacular noise of five hundred other students. Whereas I had always thought Tab odd-looking, with his moles and box-shaped head, Daniel was handsome. He was half Jewish like me and had brown hair, but he was tall, muscular, and, I thought, had a perfect face. When he would saunter to the front of the class to sharpen his pencil, I would take the opportunity to examine the details of his body: his shoulders, his legs, his blue jeans, the way he walked, the way he stood. All of these qualities seemed to flow with the pull of gravity down toward his feet into the most crowning quality of all: white leather Nikes. At the shoe store I had begged my mother to buy me those same shoes, but, unable to afford them, I was forced to settle for the canvas version, graying and fraying at the first rain.

I fantasized about being Daniel, literally, his body taking the place of mine. I was sure that the girls liked him, or loved him. The first time I was alone with him in his house, I asked him in as roundabout a manner as I could conceive: "If you were a girl, which boy in our class would you think was the best looking?"

"What do you mean, 'If I were a girl'?"

"You know, if you were still you but a girl. Who would you think would be the most handsome boy in our class?"

"It'd be me," he said, "of course."

To which I had replied candidly, too candidly, "I can see why!"

In my mind Daniel had one flaw, only one, and that was his blatant and unconcealed racism. "Last year I went trick-or-treating dressed as a nigger," he told me one day while playing in his backyard, causing me to flush, stammer, change the subject. Another time he jokingly used the word *Gerzenstein,* which he explained was a contraction of *nigger* and *Reizenstein.* And when he feigned a stomachache in gym class, it was done so as to avoid having to swim in the pool.

I overlooked all this as best I could. Evading and ignoring. Never laughing, never encouraging, and also never taking a stand. After school I would wait patiently for him in the parking lot, and when he arrived we would board his school bus together and head up into the Pittsburgh hills. In his basement we would watch television or play Ping-Pong or roll around on a big beanbag chair, the likes of which I had never experienced before. Later we would go out into his backyard, where we would join up with other boys from the neighborhood to play football. It was the waning days of October, and the leaves had changed colors and fallen from the branches and been ground into a thick paste by days of rain and boys' sneakers. It was cool but it was getting colder; winter would arrive soon. I would be turning eleven.

"Throw the ball to me, Daniel!" I would yell out. And he would throw the football and it would sail up into the late-afternoon sky, darkening toward evening, and then down, down, into my hands.

20

ON THE MORNING OF MONDAY, November 5, 1979, as my mother and I were sitting down to eat our breakfast, a peculiar report from Tehran came over National Public Radio. "Shh." The day before, a group of Iranian college students had broken off from an anti-Shah demonstration, scaled the wall of the U.S. Embassy, and taken a large group of diplomats hostage, almost all of whom were American.

I watched my mother, who was watching the radio. Her face seemed unaffected, calm almost. Was this good news? I had learned well that often what sounded like bad news was actually good news, and vice versa. I seem to remember that the broadcast did not end at the usual time but went on, moving back and forth between correspondents in the United States and Iran and Britain, each one adding to the bulk of information that was only just being unpacked.

Then it was time to leave for school, and in the middle of sounds and voices and my mother's contented demeanor, I gathered up my knapsack and my lunch.

"Good-bye, Ma," I said.

In the cafeteria that afternoon, while sitting with Daniel and Tab, I overheard a classmate mentioning to another classmate, "Did you hear what they did in Iran?" The comment was toothless and without opinion, but I registered it with displeasure. It was the first time Iran had found its way into school, and I did not approve of its appearance. I felt like pounding my fists hard on the table and upending the lunches.

On my way home after school I passed a vending machine stuffed with newspapers. The front page had a giant photo of a slightly overweight American woman, her eyes blindfolded, her mouth agape. Next to her, standing resolute and well poised, was one of her captors, a woman veiled entirely in black. Briefly, I considered trying to pry open the machine so I could remove the newspapers and dump them in the trash.

That night after dinner I sat with my mother in front of the television as we watched Walter Cronkite informing us of all that had transpired that day. The news was not good. (Or do I mean the news was good?) The television cut first to footage of Iranian men cheering and dancing maniacally around a burning American flag; then to the occupied U.S. Embassy, hung with a sign that read *Khomeini Struggles, Carter Trembles*; and then to the Iranian prime minister assuring everyone that he would be bringing a quick end to the siege. But when I awoke the next morning, the siege had not been brought to an end. During breakfast I was greeted with a report from National Public Radio that Khomeini's son had declared all ties with the United States to be severed immediately. In the cafeteria, not a word was said about Iran, but on my return home from school the afternoon paper dripped in colossal black type, U.S. HOSTAGES FACE IRAN DEATH. The use of *Iran* as a modifier added to my vexation. It seemed to imply that death was one thing, but an *Iran* death was another thing, gruesome and unimaginable.

On day four of the crisis, the prime minister's government dissolved itself, with all authority immediately being ceded to Khomeini. On day five it was discovered that one of the hostages was a twenty-two-year-old Pittsburgh woman. And a few days after that, on my way to school, I observed for the first time a yellow ribbon wrapped around a tree in front of someone's house, fluttering gently in the wind.

It will all end soon, I assured myself. Of course it will. It cannot go on forever.

But even as I thought this, I was also well aware that *I should not be desiring the end of the hostage crisis.* The taking of the embassy was a blow against imperialism, my mother had told me. It was deepening the revolution, galvanizing the masses, emboldening the Third World. Besides, the real cause of the crisis was President Carter, who had allowed the ailing Shah to enter the United States for treatment for lymphoma, an act of willful provocation. Now there was a clear and simple remedy to the dilemma: return the "Hitler of Iran," along with the seventy billion dollars he had absconded with, so that he could stand trial for his crimes against humanity. As for the breaching of diplomatic etiquette, Trotsky had already dispensed with absolute views of morality. The ends justify the means, and in the pursuit of working-class revolution, all is fair game.

"The lives of sixty-two Americans in Iran," *The Militant* declared, "are being held hostage—by the Carter administration, not by Iran."

Every evening I would sit with my mother when she watched Walter Cronkite. These were the warmest moments of my day, cozy, just the two of us, locked in against the elements. My mother would pull up the armchair in front of the television and I would, at some point in the broadcast, squeeze in beside her and lean into her body. As the cast of characters appeared on the television screen, I would ask my mother, "Good or bad?" Carter, Khomeini, Brzezinski.

"Good or bad?" I'd say to my mother. "Is he good or bad?"

"Bad," she'd say.

"What about him? That one. Is he good or bad?"

"Bad."

There was something playful about this, something like a game. According to my mother, almost everyone was bad, Americans and Iranians alike. It seemed that we were helpless and in a world without hope, where everyone was a wolf. There was hardly a single person who could be called a friend. The Americans were capitalists and the Iranians wanted to become capitalists. What made the question-and-answer so compelling for me, what made me continue asking night after night amid the endless onslaught of bad, bad, bad, was the physical rush I would get, like a gambler at the poker table, when my mother would finally respond, in reference to some new figure who appeared to make a cameo—Arafat, perhaps—"Good!"

Good! There was good, after all. It was mainly bad, yes, but there was also good. And that small dose of good, that single drop from the eyedropper, was enough to sustain me.

———

The next time Iran was mentioned in school was not in the raucous open air of the lunchroom but in the enclosed silence of my final class of the day. It was my reading class, taught by a pudgy, humorless Indian woman with a thick accent and bad breath and the improbable name of Mrs. Irani. Everyone had been working diligently at their desks, trying very quietly to map out the plot of a tedious story, when a classmate burst out with "Mrs. Irani, are you from Iran?"

The class came alive with giggles. Everyone giggled, including Daniel and Tab. I regarded their happy faces with dismay. There was perceived comedy in the prospect that someone, anyone, could actually be from Iran. Even the word itself was given the added indignity of being pronounced incorrectly, as if it were the phrase *I ran,* rather than the way my mother pronounced it, *E ron.* Again I wanted to pound my fists and shout out, not words but sound, disruptive sound, but the heavy weight of a laughing class had a sobering effect. The desire to set the record straight was replaced by a desire to leave well enough alone. I stared down at my desk, pretending to be absorbed by the story in front of me.

Mrs. Irani had not understood the question. "What did you ask?" she said, her bewilderment combined with her heavy accent causing the class to laugh again. This time louder.

"What?!" she demanded severely. "I will not have this!"

The class shushed, and the student who had first asked now affected the air of a sincere student posing a sincere question. "Are you from Iran, Mrs. Irani?" And giggles could not be suppressed.

I wondered if anyone in my class knew I was Iranian. Did Daniel and Tab know? Maybe they didn't. Maybe I had never told them. Why should I have told them when I barely considered myself Iranian in the first place? Now the ethnicity was thrust upon me all at once. There was no hiding from it. If fate had worked differently and my mother had put her foot down and named me after *her* uncle, Julius Klausner (salesman of floor coverings), I might have been sitting in Mrs. Irani's class laughing along with the other students, sheltered behind the name Julius—Julius Harris. "Stop laughing, Julius Harris!" Mrs. Irani would demand.

I stared down at the story on my desk and saw the name I had penciled in at the top of the paper come into horrible focus.

Saïd Sayrafiezadeh.

It looked up at me with wide eyes. No, do not make a sound, I thought. You must be as quiet as you can. When this is all over I will let you return.

21

On day thirteen, Khomeini did a surprising thing and ordered the immediate release of thirteen hostages, all of them black or female. This was seen by Americans as the opposite of progress. The headline of the *Pittsburgh Press* stated it plainly: IRAN HOLDS ON TO WHITE U.S. MEN. As for the future of those white men, Khomeini assured us they would be tried for espionage forthwith, and, if found guilty, he could not guarantee their safety.

Two days later President Carter ordered a naval task force to the Arabian Sea.

"Do you see what the imperialists are doing?" my mother asked.

The next day, I waited after school for Daniel and caught the bus with him as if all was normal. We played Ping-Pong in his basement until it was time to go out in the backyard. When the other boys from the neighborhood showed up, I withdrew to the edge of the grass, tossing the football stiffly.

"Saïd! Saïd!" Daniel called out, and I cringed at the sound of my name.

On day twenty, it was reported that Khomeini was proposing to train twenty million Iranians to defend the country in the event of a U.S. invasion. And that afternoon, the *Pittsburgh Press* ran a photo of a cute little blond boy, about five years old, sitting atop his father's shoulders at a rally in New Jersey. In one hand the boy held an American flag, waving it in a sea of a million other American flags; in the other hand he held a toy rifle. I knew that the boy, despite being younger than I, could overtake me, force me to the ground with ease. I would be defenseless against that little boy.

It was in December, around day forty, while everyone in class was enjoying a break before our history teacher arrived, that Daniel and I sat huddled over my desk with a piece of paper folded into a tiny triangle, pretending to play football with our fingers. The edge of the desk was the end zone, and if you managed to flick the piece of paper so that it hung just over the edge into the abyss you would have scored a touchdown. Back and forth we went, our fingers working frantically at scoring, the tiny paper football either falling short or sailing out onto the floor. And just as I was stooping to retrieve it yet again from beneath my desk, I heard Daniel ask me, "What do you think about the hostage crisis, Saïd?"

I righted myself quickly, which made all the blood rush out of my head. For a second I thought I might topple. Daniel's face appeared composed and unperturbed. He must have thought it was a throwaway question, more small talk than inquest. It was certainly asked with ease.

"Let's bomb Iran," I thought to say. How simple that would be. Just a quick retort. I could feel the words right at the tip of my tongue. "Let's bomb Iran, Daniel. That's what I think. How about you?" "I think the same thing, Saïd." Then we would finish our game of paper football. But the thing that had gripped me one year earlier at Victor's dinner table with his father gripped me again. The orator rose. I saw him rising and I was helpless to stop him. He entered the stage, took his place behind the podium, and said to the audience, "I believe the hostages are spies and should be tried for their crimes against the Iranian people." And on top of that, indulgently, speaking long after the applause had ended, he added, "They'll deserve whatever they get."

Daniel stared at me. Perhaps he was trying to ascertain whether or not I was kidding. *Just kidding, Daniel. Ha-ha.* I could feel a fog settling around us. Mr. Petrisko entered the room, bald and eyeglassed, and I watched Daniel turn to his desk and open his book. He moved slowly, like he was made of clay. Everything was slow. Even Mr. Petrisko's voice was slow. "Let's stop all the chitchat," he said to the class.

The following day Daniel did not speak to me. I knew immediately that I was in trouble, but I chose to cling to other, more-hopeful versions of events.

"Are you sick, Daniel?"

"What did you say?"

"Are you sick?"

He wasn't sick. In the lunchroom I could see him over at the other table laughing freely with Tab. What were they laughing about? Maybe I was the one who was sick. Yes, I was not feeling too well. With my uneaten lunch I navigated my way, stumbling, groping, to the bathroom. I ran my hands under the cold water. In the mirror I observed the features of my face. *Your eyebrows are like his.* The eyebrows rested thickly over my eyes. Is that how eyebrows are supposed to look?

The next day at school, Daniel's back seemed to always be facing toward me. And now Tab's back was turned. "Are you sick, Tab?" The next day too. Had it now been three days of silence?

And then I did a terrible thing, a desperate thing. "Hey, Daniel," I said. We were sitting in math class but it hadn't begun yet. "Hey, Daniel, I was watching *Saturday Night Live* and one of the actors—I can't remember his name—one of the actors was pretending to be from South Africa and he was talking about the Krugerrand, but instead of saying 'Krugerrand,' he was saying 'niggerand.' Isn't that funny, Daniel? Niggerand." How simple, how easy. And Daniel smiled.

"Daniel, do you want me to come over to your house today?" I asked. "I thought we could play Ping-Pong." I could hear the sound of pleading in my voice.

"Oh, sure. Okay."

Okay? Yes! Okay. He had said it. There, see, the fog was lifting. There was nothing to be worried about. He had been sick but now he was well. And when the bell rang to end the day, I gathered my books and rushed to the parking lot to wait for him to come and collect me. As I stood there, I observed the white students boarding their yellow buses. Each with their books and their bags. A horde of white students, one after the other. Beyond them were the black students as they went their own way. Then the yellow bus doors closed. I looked for Daniel in the crowd but could not see him. Perhaps we had missed each other and now he was already sitting on the bus, hoping I'd come. But which bus was his bus?

"Is Daniel on this bus?" I yelled to the driver.

"Who?"

And when the bus pulled away, I saw that all the buses were pulling away. I stood alone in the parking lot and watched them go. A row of giant yellow animals. Still I waited. Eventually the teachers came out the side doors, carrying their papers and their books, and they walked to their cars and also left for the day.

How immense the parking lot looked when there was nothing in it. The trees cast long shadows.

It had been a mistake, of course. A mix-up. He had been waiting for me, and I had let him down. Oh, well, we will try again tomorrow. But when I started to squeeze through the fence in the direction of my apartment, I suddenly saw so vividly the Ping-Pong table and the beanbag chair and the backyard, and without considering what I was doing I began to walk the other way.

I followed the path that his school bus would take, meandering through the city streets, curving and winding block by block as if tracking a trail of bread crumbs. I trekked up steep hills and then down steep hills—Pittsburgh is a city of hills. It was getting dusky. I was losing time. Will we have time to play in the backyard? My legs ached and I grew thirsty. I walked on. Daniel will be surprised to see me when I arrive. He will be happy to see me.

"I was getting worried," he will say.

It was evening when I arrived at his front door. I could

hear the sound of voices coming from somewhere, boys' voices. Laughter. I pressed the bell and the door opened.

"Hey, Daniel," I said with good cheer.

His face went pale to see me.

"I missed your bus," I said. "Sorry about that."

He shrugged and turned without a word—was he sick?— and I followed him through his grand home and then outside into the backyard, where I joined the other boys already at play.

"Throw the ball to me, Daniel!" I shouted at the top of my lungs, but now there was no time, because I had arrived too late and it was already night.

And the next day in school it was all laid bare when Mrs. Irani distributed a piece of paper to each of us. "This is a homework assignment," she announced, her Indian accent causing the words *homework* and *assignment* to bounce up and down like rubber balls. Listed on the paper were a series of sentences, and within each sentence was the name of a country. Australia, Spain, Japan, etc. And Iran. What were we supposed to do with the names of these countries in each of these sentences?

"I will explain in a moment," Mrs. Irani said, but before she could explain, Daniel rose from his seat like a lawyer objecting to the judge and declared with mock outrage for all to hear, "Iran is on this paper!" Then, looking directly at me, he held the paper up by the tips of his fingers as if it were a thing that had rotted in the sun. "Burn it!" he shouted to me. "Burn the paper!"

There was tittering and twittering in the class. Tab turned and looked at me with eager eyes.

"Burn the paper!" Daniel said.

"Burn it!" someone else said.

"Bomb it!" Daniel said.

"What?!" Mrs. Irani said. "I will not have this in my class!" But in the noisy confusion she thought only that her students were angry about having been given a homework assignment.

My classmates' faces floated around me, fleshy and white, distorted with laughter, like gargoyles on the side of a building. A school of gargoyles, a city, a country.

"I will explain the assignment in a moment!" Mrs. Irani shouted. But there was no one anywhere who could hear her voice.

22

My mother continued to listen to National Public Radio at breakfast, but I ceased watching her expression. I assumed, as a matter of course, that the news would do me no good. On my walk to school, I would pass the American flags and the yellow ribbons and the bumper stickers of Mickey Mouse giving Iran the middle finger. I no longer paused at the vending machine to look at the day's headlines, as today's headlines could not be distinguished from yesterday's headlines. Once inside the walls of school, I did my best to stay as still as possible, to look at no one, to engage no one, praying that my quietude would encourage quietude in others. I had gone beyond expecting ever to be included again by Daniel or Tab or anyone else and instead sat in the back of the classroom, resigned to my fate, my gaze fixed at the center of my desk, hoping I would not be called on, hoping that current events would not be discussed, hoping that we would not have a substitute teacher that day who would mispronounce my name, bringing full focus once again to the fact that there was an Iranian in our midst. In the evening, I would still sit with my mother and watch Walter Cronkite, but I no longer asked, "Good or bad?" "And that's the way it is," he would say, "Wednesday, January sixteenth, 1980." Now amended to include the coda, "The seventy-third day of captivity for the American hostages in Iran."

One morning, going first as I always did to my locker to put away my lunch and to retrieve my books, I heard Daniel's familiar voice behind me, close to my ear, saying "I bet he won't fight."

I was kneeling on the carpeted floor and I had the impulse to stand and turn, but then Tab's voice joined in: "No, he won't fight."

"They're too scared to fight."

"They're all cowards."

"They're yellow."

"They've got yellow streaks running down their backs."

"Look at that yellow streak running down his back."

It was a bizarre, antiquated taunt. Something from another era. I continued to rummage through my locker as if I could not find the thing I needed. The fact that I was on my hands and knees while they stood above me added to the tableau of submission. I had knelt of my own accord, but it felt like I had been forced. To stand would imply a willingness to confront them, and that was not something I wanted to do. So I stayed on my knees, and let them carry on until the bell rang for our class to begin.

Daniel continued to remain handsome in my eyes. In fact, he became more handsome, while I, in turn, became more ugly. This was the unhappy side effect of having first perceived him as my flawless opposite. I grew skinnier, frailer, as he grew more strapping. My features became loud and prominent while his became refined and elegant. I was sure that he would be a movie star when he grew up. It was as if my face was cannibalizing the flesh from my body, absorbing it into itself, so that my nose and eyes and eyebrows intensified with each day, growing darker, larger, hairier. It was a hideous face, I was sure, loudly calling attention to itself. Now I avoided the mirror at all costs.

And one afternoon in the lunchroom, as I ate quietly among boys who did not know my name or where I came from, I was approached by a white student, a scholar from another class, whom I knew only vaguely. His name was Alan, and he was short and intelligent and Jewish, and he had an impressive vocabulary, having once astonished me by using the word *literally* in a sentence. "The teacher literally stood up and . . ."

"Hey, Saïd," Alan said. "Come with me, I want to show you something funny."

I was surprised to be invited, and I stuffed my uneaten lunch into my brown paper bag and followed Alan toward the edge of the lunchroom where I could see a dozen boys standing in a circle. I wondered suddenly where he was taking me and why I had agreed to follow so unquestioningly. But I had conceived of these questions too late and could not now turn back. When we were just a few yards from the circle it opened dramatically, like a claw, and in the center stood Daniel. His shoulders and chest looked broader than they had before, his hands and forearms thicker, a boy in a man's body. I could feel the energy of the boys in the circle, many of whom I knew only tangentially. Daniel looked at me and I looked away. Where were the teachers? The din of the lunchroom swelled. I watched as Alan, who had invited me there, now crossed into the open claw and took his place beside Daniel, the two facing out at me. The thought of raising my arms to fight panicked me. I will allow myself to be beaten, I thought. That is what I will do. It will be easier that way, faster. I will fall. My lunch will spill. My pants will tear. Then it will be over. *I'm yellow.*

"If you were a girl," Alan asked Daniel, turning to him and projecting his voice like an actor onstage, "which boy in our class would you think was the best looking?"

And Daniel said, like he was also an actor responding to his cue: "It'd be me, of course."

To which Alan replied, "I can see why!"

The heat in my chest rushed into my face as the boys erupted in laughter. The circle closed. I stayed on the periphery, pulled in by its orbit, listening to the high, friendly chatter. I waited for it to reopen, but the role I had been cast in was no longer needed.

And that night I told my mother.

"They're bothering me at school, Ma."

It was a shameful thing to admit.

My mother was in the living room, sitting on her bed, and she leaned forward, her eyebrows creased with concern.

"Who's bothering you?"

"Boys," I said generally. "Boys."

"What boys?"

"Boys in school."

"In your class?" Her voice rose. Her fingers intertwined.

"I guess so."

"Why are they bothering you, Saïd?"

"I don't know."

"What do you mean, you don't know?"

"I don't know."

"Did you do something?"

"I think they're bothering me because I'm Iranian, Ma."

And at the word *Iranian,* my mother's eyebrows unknit themselves and a void spread across her face. We looked at each other for a while. Was there something more I was supposed to say? And then my mother nodded, a short nod, as if to say "You are excused." I went into the bedroom and waited for her to come and let me know what she was going to do next. When I was in second grade a teacher had referred to the class as "a pack of wild Indians," and my mother had written a letter of complaint that I was made to hand-deliver. But when she called me now it was because supper was ready, and at supper the subject was not raised. Nor was it raised the next day.

And so in lieu of any assistance I took to carrying a little piece of metal that I had found on the floor of occupational/vocational training. It was about the size of a paper clip, with a sharp, jagged end, and I was determined, if ever there was cause, to poke my assailant in the eye. I knew I would never actually be brave enough to do this, but the thought of doing it empowered me. When I sat at my desk, when I walked the halls between classes, when I ate my lunch, I would finger the piece of metal in my pocket, and I would feel soothed by its presence.

23

MEANWHILE, IN IRAN, MAHMOUD SAYRAFIEZADEH and his recently renamed Revolutionary Workers Party—so as to distinguish themselves from the faction calling itself the Militant Wing of the Socialist Workers Party—were diligently preparing for the first presidential election in the history of the nation. One hundred twenty-four candidates registered for this historic event that would finally, irrevocably, bring an end to twenty-five centuries of monarchy. The dream that Saïd Salmasi had fought and died for had finally come to pass, and my father, having lived his life under the shadow of such sacrifice, respectfully accepted his party's nomination.

Born in Tabriz in the year 1313 A.H.

Author of the book *Nationality and Revolution in Iran*

Twenty-five years of struggle against the Shah while in exile

Mahmoud Sayrafiezadeh for President

The cover of an accompanying manifesto showed Jimmy Carter's head either resting on or emerging from a giant pile of skulls. And escaping into Carter's gaping, yawning mouth was a diminutive version of the Shah clutching a suitcase in each hand, presumably stuffed with seventy billion dollars in cash.

"The presidential elections are being held," the campaign platform read,

> while U.S. imperialism is prolonging its economic blockade, hoping that aggressive military action and political attacks will help to regain its all-out hegemony over this country. In pursuance of the diabolical plan, U.S. imperialists have mobilized all of their international allies and agents, including the United Nations and domestic capitalists. They long for the return of the Pahlavi reign, militarism, autocracy, and the consolidation of capitalists' ascendancy in order that they will suppress the workers' and peasants' campaign for liberty and deliverance from poverty . . .

Against this unhappy end, my father proposed a half dozen solutions, the first and foremost of which was support for the "anti-imperialist campaign" being waged by the Muslim Students Following the Line of the Imam, who continued to hold fifty-three Americans hostage.

I learned about my father's candidacy by way of another envelope that arrived for me just a week after my eleventh birthday. "Here you are," my mother said again. Inside, I found a leaflet written entirely in Persian, with densely packed text on both sides, much of it black, some of it red. Next to the text was a small, closely cropped photo of my father's clean-shaven face, with that same inviting, confident smile. There was no note included, no explanation, no translation, and except for the fact that someone had written *For Saïd* at the very top of the leaflet, there was nothing to indicate that it was actually for me. It was a leaflet, after all, printed and distributed for the multitudes. Still, it felt like an acknowledgment of sorts for my birthday—if not a gift, then a sound reason for there not being a gift.

I sat for a few minutes at the edge of my bed with the wincing understanding that the news of my father's candidacy was spectacular and that any other boy would be proud of it. So instead of putting the leaflet in my sock drawer, I thumbtacked it next to a picture of John Travolta on the bulletin board above my desk for all to admire. Here I was, in possession of a powerful secret that would astonish the world if it were ever to find out. It was so enticing and irresistible a secret, in fact, that when Mr. Petrisko announced to the class that we were each to bring in something to present for current events, I hesitated not at all and chose the leaflet. Not until I was sitting in the back of the classroom, watching the students stand and deliver, did I understand how absolutely compromised I had made myself. In front of me on my desk sat the leaflet, and in front of the leaflet sat Daniel and Tab and an entire room of likeminded boys and girls. I watched with growing apprehension as each student took center stage and proceeded to teach us about what was going on with things like the state of the steel industry in Pittsburgh. My relief each time Iran was not mentioned was counterbalanced by the knowledge that I was the one who was going to be doing the mentioning. I thought for a moment of crumpling up the leaflet and claiming I had misunderstood the assignment, but that seemed beyond forgivable.

Finally it was my turn to present. There was no getting around it. I stood and walked to the front of the class, my knees barely bending, and took the spotlight. I held the leaflet gingerly in front of me, with my other hand deep in my pocket fingering the small piece of metal. I looked out into the rows of faces that ran from disinterested to murderous, judiciously avoiding Daniel's and Tab's.

"This is a leaflet for someone who is running for president of Iran," I said. Then I waited. What was I waiting for? I was waiting for someone to ask me who the man in the leaflet was.

This is a leaflet for someone who is running for president of Iran.

Who is the man in the leaflet, Saïd?

To freely offer that he was my father felt like cheating. So I waited. And the class waited. And Mr. Petrisko waited. And I realized, standing there in a sea of silence, that I had nothing whatsoever else to say about the leaflet in my hand. It began and ended with my father. My gaze dropped from the faces in front to my shoes below, the gray canvas Nikes. Then I studied the carpeting. It was such soft carpeting, and I wondered what it would be like to take a nap on it.

Soon I heard Mr. Petrisko's voice waking me, asking, "Can you tell the class something about the language the leaflet's written in, Saïd?"

I looked at him. I blanched. I did not know anything about the language the leaflet was written in. The language was beside the point.

"Can you tell the class something about the history of Iran, Saïd?"

I saw that I was trapped in a student–teacher exchange from which there was no exit. I stood in front of the class, undressed, tilting to one side, examining the leaflet as if I was just about to say something interesting, fully aware that I had failed the assignment. Under the bright lights of the classroom, the quality of the leaflet appeared to me as shoddy and amateurish, a thing you might find at a community center. Why hadn't I noticed that before? The single hole I had made with the thumbtack looked at me.

"Okay, Saïd, thank you," Mr. Petrisko said, mercifully giving me permission to take my seat. Which I did at once. Returning again to the piece of steel in my pocket, while I watched the next student rise and begin to effortlessly expound on the debate over nuclear power. "This is a photograph of Three Mile Island . . ."

When class was over I stayed behind, hovering around Mr. Petrisko's desk until he was done shuffling his papers.

"I just wanted to tell you," I said, once we were alone, "that the man in the leaflet is Mahmoud Sayrafiezadeh."

He looked at me without effect.

"He's my father," I said.

I said it with understatement, with false humility, so that Mr. Petrisko would have room for his response.

Why didn't you say something, Saïd? That changes every-thing.

"Is that so?" he said, with an understatement that equaled mine.

"Yes," I said.

Then neither of us said anything, because there was nothing else to say, and soon Mr. Petrisko returned to the mound of papers on his desk.

24

MY FATHER LOST, ANYWAY. MORE than fourteen million people went to the polls in Iran, and eleven million of them cast their ballot for Abolhassan Bani-Sadr. Ahmad Madani took about two million, Hassan Habib five hundred thousand, and the remaining sixty or so candidates—another sixty had already dropped out by the time of the election—divided up what was left. The fight for a socialist Iran had been stalled.

A week or so after I presented the leaflet, I was sitting in English class taking a test on verbs and nouns when the door opened and a classmate I had once been friendly with entered the room. Everyone automatically looked up to see who could be so late for class, and when we did we saw Charlie, with his faded jeans and his dirty-blond hair and a black T-shirt with a grotesque caricature of Khomeini's face—all eyebrows and nose—in the center of a bull's-eye. Above the bull's-eye, in giant white letters, were two simple words: *Iran Sucks.*

There was a clean space of silence as fifty eyes in the room absorbed the meaning of what was emblazoned on the boy's chest, absorbed that a boy could indeed be so bold as to wear it to class, and when it was all fully processed every mouth in the room opened up and laughed. It had the timbre of a shriek, high-pitched and prolonged. Add to it that the fifty eyes had now turned away from the bull's-eye and on to me, keenly seeking my reaction. I sat in my chair, thinking *I support the struggle of the Iranian workers and peasants against U.S. imperialism. . . .*

The class was taught by a tall pretty blonde who I had a crush on, and she waited until the sound had all but died away before suggesting, respectfully, that the boy go and put a jacket on. "That's not an appropriate shirt to wear to school, Charlie," she said with a boys-will-be-boys tone that infuriated me. Charlie dutifully departed, but when he returned wearing a plain brown jacket, it elicited its own squeals of delight. Beneath it, we all knew, resided a terribly tantalizing thing. The thrill was now in what was unspoken. And throughout the rest of the day, whenever a teacher stepped out of the classroom or turned to the chalkboard, Charlie would stand and unzip his jacket, exposing his chest defiantly, delighting the classroom. "Tell me what is so funny!" Mrs. Irani exclaimed, which made everyone laugh even more.

I resolved finally to do what my mother could not do, and I asked Mr. Petrisko to move me into another class. He didn't ask me why and I didn't tell him why, but I knew he knew. Since there was only one "scholars" class on my floor, there was nowhere to put me except into the class known as "regular." I agreed to it immediately, and the following Monday, not a day too soon, I took my seat in a room filled with black boys and girls, where I instantly reverted back to a white child.

And that is where I stayed for the remainder of the school year, quietly, anonymously, doing work without challenge, but entirely content. The only time I was noticed was when there was a substitute teacher, who would mangle my name and everyone would laugh. Other than that, my classmates barely paid attention to me. Even that April, when the helicopters crashed in the desert in an attempt to rescue the hostages, Iran was not mentioned. I made no friends in that class, but that was okay. I no longer had any interest in making friends.

25

THINGS DID NOT GO WELL for my father after he lost the presidential election. And things did not go well for Iran. The balance of power, already weighted heavily in favor of the clerics and Khomeini, tipped further. A cultural revolution surged through the country, and vestiges of the West—including neckties—were banned, journalists were imprisoned for criticizing Islam, and women were ordered to wear the veil in public, reversing the previous five decades where women had been ordered *not* to wear the veil in public. Universities became engulfed in deadly riots. Thousands were hanged or shot for the crime of counterrevolution. The Mujahideen, with a guerrilla army of a hundred thousand, fought back against the government with bombings and assassinations. Reprisals followed reprisals. Unemployment soared. To make matters worse, Saddam Hussein bombed the Mehrabad Airport on September 22, 1980, blacking out Tehran and beginning a war that would last eight years and take a million lives. And, of course, there were the hostages.

Even the Revolutionary Workers Party—which had already split from the Socialist Workers Party of Iran—was beset by more discord and disagreement, and sixty members broke off to found the Workers Unity Party. The party printed its own newspaper, *Hemmat (Determination),* with my father as editor, and a platform that claimed it was the only party *which shows the road to victory for the working class.* What Barnes had triumphantly proclaimed just two years earlier as "the first Trotskyist party on Iranian soil" was now three Trotskyist parties on Iranian soil, opposing Islam and one another while struggling for relevance in a country that was descending into chaos. My father did not stop advocating for his vision of Iran, softened now to include critical support for the clerics, but, even so, the space for dissent was growing more narrow by the day.

The Socialist Workers Party in the United States continued to support the revolution, arguing that while it might be Islamic it was also anti-imperialist and that it should be defended without condition. But there was no mistaking that the enthusiasm had worn away and the time had come to move on. It was not going to be the revolution we had hoped for. My mother still listened to National Public Radio every morning, pausing as she always did when the news turned to Iran, but now she listened without reproach or recrimination. And my father was no longer mentioned in our household. There was nothing more to say about him, really. It was just the two of us once again, my mother and me, sitting together at the kitchen table.

By the time I started seventh grade, the hostage crisis was well into its tenth month. I had been returned to the scholars class, but I was prepared my first day to ask to be transferred straight into regular if need be. There would be no delay this time. Much to my relief, however, an influx of new students had shuffled things, and by the luck of the draw Daniel and Tab had been placed far away on another floor. And as for the students in my classroom, Iran had ceased to be an urgent topic of conversation. It scarcely mattered, though, as I had already made up my mind that under no circumstance would I make my opinion known. Furthermore, I had devised the clever strategy of telling anyone who inquired that I was Persian. No one, including me, knew exactly where or what Persia was, but everyone seemed satisfied with the answer.

I saw Daniel and Tab rarely, one of the benefits to being in a school of two thousand, but when I did, the old panic would rush back into me, all the feelings of humiliation and docility and betrayal, fresh and clear, and I would escape down another hall. Years later, just before graduating from high school, I happened to run into Daniel at a party. He was drunk when he saw me, and it took him a moment to register who I was. Finally he exclaimed, "Saïd!" As if we were long-lost friends. "How have you been, Saïd?"

"I've been fine" is all I said.

And I watched him wobble back against the wall, start to say something more, lose the words, start again, but before he could put the sentence together I had already hurried past him out the door.

The hostages were finally released on January 20, 1981, after four hundred forty-four days of captivity. I had been ten years old that November morning I stood in the living room listening to National Public Radio report their capture. Now

I was twelve. The principal interrupted class to deliver the news. "Attention all students and teachers," he said over the loudspeaker, obviously excited to have his moment to shine. But his announcement was imbued with anticlimax, and the class seemed to receive it with vague indifference.

And not long after that, in the privacy of my bedroom, I removed my father's presidential leaflet from the bulletin board. It seemed like a relic from a bygone era, and its presence served only as a constant reminder that there was no longer any word from him. Into the empty rectangle of space I thumbtacked what had become the foremost issue of the times for the party: an illustration of a despairing American soldier, head in hands, sitting next to the grave where his brother-in-arms had just been buried. *No Draft. No War. U.S. out of El Salvador. Vote Socialist Workers.* As for my father's leaflet, I carefully folded it back into thirds and placed it in my sock drawer, alongside his letter. It was only his photograph that remained, hovering above my bed, fixed and immovable. The rest of him was gone.

26

THAT SUMMER OF 1981 I went to Cuba. "Now you'll be able to see socialism firsthand," my mother said. The tour was being organized by the Socialist Workers Party and was billed as a possible final time that the U.S. government would permit travel to the island. (Which actually ended up being true.)

I tried to act like I was excited about going, but I wasn't. The prospect of spending a week in a strange place without my mother perturbed me. Plus the only way to get to Cuba was to fly out of Miami—approximately a thirty-minute flight—but in order to get to Miami I had to ride on a Greyhound bus for twenty hours. I also realized that in order for my mother to send me on a trip that cost seven hundred dollars, she must have had a lot more money than she admitted.

A week before I was to leave, my mother and I sat down to a supper of spaghetti and meatballs. It was by far my favorite meal, and it helped to break the monotony of a consistent diet comprised almost exclusively of frozen peas, white rice, and bread and butter. No sooner had we begun to eat than my mother launched into yet another cheerful monologue about everything I was going to see and experience in Cuba. And without giving any thought to what I was saying, I blurted out in the middle of a mouthful of spaghetti, "I hope the United States bombs Cuba!"

My mother's face went ashen. Then her eyes filled with

tears. Yellow Castro stared down at me from the bulletin board. I realized in an instant the tremendous power of my words, their unbearable weight. There was a moment of calm silence, but it was a false calm, as when a gentle wind blowing across a meadow signifies an approaching storm. Then my mother exhaled.

"Don't you ever say that!" She screamed this, and at the top of her lungs. I thought immediately of our neighbors. "Don't you ever say that!"

I recanted immediately. "I'm sorry, Ma!"

My apology went unheeded. "Don't you ever say that!"

"It was a joke," I said, and I tried to laugh as if we were merely dealing in misunderstanding.

"Don't you ever joke about that!"

"Really, I'm sorry, Ma. I won't joke. I promise I won't joke."

"Don't you ever joke!" Louder still.

"I won't joke, Ma."

Then there was quiet. Anger replaced by dismay. Only time could heal the wound between us. I looked down at my plate of red spaghetti, red like blood, and I wondered how I could have gone so wrong. I also wondered if it was possible to begin eating again or if I would be seen as being not only callous but gluttonous as well. "Look at the rich asses stuffing their faces at a time like this!" Not to eat, however, would be elongating the crisis, so I picked up my fork and dug it tentatively into the food. My mother said nothing. I took a bite. I waited for her to respond. She did not. I took another bite. I waited. Then my mother picked up her fork and together we ate our spaghetti.

I arrived in Havana at night. It was very dark and very warm, a soggy warmth that I had never experienced before and that added to the stultifying twenty-four hours of travel. My clothes clung to my skin and my feet felt swollen. There were dozens of other comrades and sympathizers along on the tour, but I had something of a personal chaperone, a burly blond man named Paul, who was new to the party and I didn't know well but to whom my mother had felt comfortable entrusting my welfare. We all climbed into a van and were driven about an hour out of Havana to our beach resort. All the cars on the street were antiques, like toys. "The effects of the imperialist embargo," one of the comrades said. Next to me sat a boy named Roger. He was sixteen and about to join the Young Socialist Alliance. I listened while he talked to the adults about Cuban politics. Everyone sounded so excited to finally be here that my overriding emotions of exhaustion and disinterest were brought into high relief. I felt a growing sense of impatience and irritation toward myself, as if one part of me was scolding the other part of me. The adventure was just beginning for the comrades, but here I was already missing my mother and wanting to be back home. I knew this was the thought of a child and that I had been sent on this trip precisely because I had been deemed mature enough. To act like a child now would be to fail at some very important test and waste my mother's money.

That night at dinner, glasses of water with pink and purple umbrellas were set in front of everyone. I happily put the umbrella in my pocket, but when I sipped the water, it seared my mouth and I gasped out loud.

"That's rum," Roger said. "If you don't want it, I'll take it."

No, I thought, I'm going to drink it. That's what I'm going to do. I sipped again and my mouth caught fire again.

A waiter put a plate of chicken and vegetables in front of me. I ate and drank. I'm going to eat and drink everything! My head swirled. I thought about my mother and what she might be doing at that exact moment and if she would be angry with me if she knew I was drinking rum or if she would say that I was having an adventure.

"Can I have your umbrella?" I asked Roger.

"I want mine," he said.

"Can I have your umbrella?" I asked the comrade next to me.

"Of course, Saïd."

I put it in my pocket.

The next morning, before we headed off on our first excursion, I stood on the beach with my knapsack and a headache and watched blue waves gently rolling in and out. The sand was soft and the sun hung low over the horizon and everything looked beautiful. "Just ninety miles off the coast of imperialism," everyone was fond of saying. Roger came running by in a bathing suit. "There's still time to go swimming," he said. Then he splashed into the water. "The water's perfect!" I watched his head go under. The last time I had been on a beach was when I still lived in Brooklyn. My mother had landed a job one summer working for the National Opinion Research Center, which required her to canvass large swaths of area. Each weekend the two of us would take the subway out to Coney Island, where I would play in the sand on the edge of the ocean while my mother walked around asking sunbathers personal questions. I knew how much she loathed the job, how demoralized she was by it, and I always felt bad for her. One day on the beach we had become separated, and in my barefoot confusion I stepped on a burning cigarette and instantly crumpled to the ground. A strange man saw that I was in need and knelt down and scooped me up into his arms.

The first stop on our tour of Cuba was a cigar factory. I had never been in a factory before and I was mortified by what I saw. It was dark and dirty and hot, much hotter than outside even, and it smelled of a thick, heavy tobacco sweetness that nauseated me. I could not imagine surviving more than an hour inside the factory, let alone the eight, ten, twelve hours that the workers spent there each day as they picked their way through great mountains of tobacco. Roger and all the comrades, however, thought everything was great, being able to look past the external discomfort and see a fair and equitable workplace like none that existed in the United States. We crowded together in the stifling heat, passing around a tin cup filled with water, while comrades asked questions of the workers, which would then be translated into Spanish. I was bored out of my mind and didn't care about anything that was being asked or answered. But when everyone laughed at something, I laughed, and when everyone turned grave, so did I. I kept thinking that I should ask a question so that everyone would be impressed with me, but I had no idea what that question should be. Our guide told an anecdote about how Castro had once proclaimed that a single Cuban life was worth more than all the tobacco fields in Cuba, and I pictured a Cuban being kidnapped by the United States and Castro then burning all the fields so that he could get that Cuban back. At the very end of the discussion, Roger raised his hand and asked the guide how he could go about moving to Cuba. Everyone laughed—including me—and then we shook our heads wistfully.

The sugarcane farm we visited played out the same. Questions, answers, and complete admiration. And so did the random person's living room we sat in for two hours. And so did everywhere else we visited on our tour. But for me, fifteen minutes could not pass without my mind becoming preoccupied with how hot I was, or how thirsty I was, or what my mother might be doing. I was also terribly concerned about misplacing, losing, or confusing the three forms of currency I carried with me at all times, and so I had devised a system of putting my traveler's checks in one pocket, my Cuban pesos in another, and my American dollars in a third. During the various tours and discussions I would find myself repeatedly tapping first my back pocket, then my left, then my right.

Outpacing all other concerns, however, was my fear of having to go to the bathroom. One of the first observations I made about Cuba was that the public restrooms were filthy and decrepit, generally without toilet paper or toilet seats, and overrun with flies, even in the restaurants. I knew that the effects of the U.S. embargo against Cuba were reflected in these restrooms and that I should be above such pedestrian concerns, but I was not. I was constantly hounded by the prospect of having to go, and I would do my best to hold on until I returned to the resort at the end of the day. When that proved unfeasible, I would rush at the last possible moment to the nearest restroom, where I would hover uncomfortably above the seatless bowl.

As the days passed, my frustration with myself mounted, exacerbated by everyone's outsize enthusiasm, especially Roger's. I began to entertain thoughts of joining the Young Socialist Alliance myself. That would dazzle my mother upon my return and make her think the money well spent. I was twelve, but twelve wasn't too young to join, my sister, after all, had become a member when she was eleven or twelve. Besides, it was my destiny. Wasn't I to one day be a great revolutionary like my father? I had always assumed so, as had everyone else. One night in the loneliness of my mother's apartment I had passed the time by staring at my reflection in the living-room window and making my face look the way I thought a revolutionary's face should look, proud and solemn, like Castro's when he had been brought to trial by Batista. "History will absolve me!" he had told the courtroom. For a long while I stood there, trying to get the features of my face just right, imagining that many people were looking at me and that they were all applauding.

In the middle of the week we went to Havana by way of a public bus, which was long in coming and completely filled when it arrived. A Cuban man stood and gave his seat to one of the female comrades. Even as the bus emptied, the man continued to stand, allowing everyone else the opportunity to sit. All the comrades were really happy with the man, and some of them spoke Spanish to him. I understood that the man's generous behavior was not because of his personality but because of the revolution. That the revolution had created a new, selfless kind of person, a kind of person that no one had really ever known before. At La Plaza de la Revolución, an enormous portrait of Che hung from the side of a building, and my earlier declaration—"I hope the United States bombs Cuba!"—resounded in my ears, shaming me until I felt fully and unconditionally cured. Children my age held out their hands, begging for candy. "Chiclets! Chiclets!" they pleaded. For some reason all the comrades had said never to give them anything, and so I cruelly ignored them and wandered into shops, trying to find a gift for my mother. I wondered what she would look like when I saw her again.

The day before we were to leave, a group of Cuban children gathered around us at the beach resort and we had an impromptu discussion regarding Cuban society. It was obvious that all the comrades were impressed not just with the answers the children gave but also with the sophisticated way in which they gave them. Here were yet more examples of the kind of person—the kind of *children*—a socialist revolution could create. I seethed at the attention they were getting and the way they elicited both laughter and sympathy from the comrades. And, as I had done every time before, I racked my brain for a question that would make people impressed with me also. Eventually I tugged at the interpreter's arm and asked her to ask the children if it was common for Cuban teachers to beat them in school. I asked it in a certain underplayed way that I hoped would imply that, while it was a very important question for me to ask, it was also a very difficult question for me to ask, because *I* was being beaten by my teachers in school. That way I could engender both pity for having to live in the United States as well as praise for being brave enough to speak up and reveal its dark side. I had the added satisfaction of having the interpreter pretend to slap me so that she could better illustrate the meaning of the question to the children.

"No," one of the boys answered, looking at me indifferently, as if he could not be bothered with such questions.

"No," the interpreter translated for me.

When my plane landed in Miami, I had to go to the bathroom. Once again dread came over me, and I entered the airport restroom with trepidation. I was flabbergasted by what I saw: The restroom was spotless and bright. A wall of mirrors amplified the shininess. There was also air-conditioning. I chose a stall and found to my great relief both toilet paper and toilet seat. How absolutely happy I was to be back in the United States. How thankful. And while I thought this, I knew—as I have many times in my life—that this was the wrong thought to be having.

27

THE IVY ON THE PLAYGROUND fence had grown thick that summer. I noticed it in the afternoons on my way home from school or while running an errand for my mother. Even though it was fall, it looked to still be climbing higher. Through it I could see boys my age playing baseball or football, shouting and running. Many of these boys I recognized from Reizenstein—some black, some white—but they were in other grades or other classes and I didn't know their names. From the way they played, it looked like they had been friends for years, and I assumed they had attended the neighborhood elementary school together, whereas I, of course, had been bused an hour across the city. Sometimes I would think about entering the playground and joining these boys, but I had no real idea how to go about that, and so I would go back home, eat a snack, do my homework, and wait for my mother to return from work.

On my way back from the grocery store one afternoon, about a month into my eighth-grade year, I paused just at the edge of the playground to watch as the boys took turns throwing a tennis ball against the brick wall. It was a variation of the game I had played alone in my backyard where I had imagined that I was Reggie Jackson hitting the ball and then also fielding the ball. Standing on the periphery holding a grocery bag with a loaf of bread, I watched the action for a while, unobserved. "I got it!" they screamed with their arms outstretched, each of them hoping to be the one to catch the prize. At one point, two black men dressed in work boots and the checkered pants of short-order cooks passed through with a basketball, interrupting the game.

"Hurry up!" one of the boys brazenly yelled out, and in response the cooks slowed further, sauntering leisurely with exaggerated strides.

"Is this fast enough for you, little man?" they called back, causing everyone to break out into laughter.

Soon a boy arrived with a baseball bat, and the group decided that they would now play a real game of baseball. But, after having divided themselves up, they saw that the boy with the bat had made them an odd number and that of course he would not be willing to sit out, nor would anyone else be willing to sit out. It was then that one of the boys turned and saw me standing by the fence.

"Do you want to play?" he asked.

The boy stared at me, expectation written across his face. The others waited too. Beyond them I could see the cooks dribbling up and down the basketball court.

"I have a loaf of bread," I said, thinking they would understand, but even as I said it I felt my hand release the bag. I heard the sound of the thump of the bread as it dropped to the ground.

I should go home, I thought.

"I'll play," I said.

And so into the evening I scampered across the concrete, chasing after a bouncing tennis ball until it was time for the boy with the bat to go home. And when I arrived at the playground the next afternoon, earlier than the day before, I hesitated only a moment before entering the fray and competing for that elusive ball as if it were mine by right. When it rained the following day, steady and light, I did not despair but remained in the playground with the other boys, skidding recklessly over the wet surface, throwing caution to the wind. By the time I collided with a boy named Eric and fell hard to the ground, I had become a part of the fabric of the neighborhood. "Holy shit, Saïd!" the others screamed. Eric was a year older than me but shorter, with curly hair and pigeon toes, and he had a white mother and a black father. He also had a younger brother, and in their bedroom later that day we reenacted the scene, now done in slow motion, twisting and falling onto the bed. Then the three of us sat on the couch in the living room, watching movies on cable television and gorging ourselves on peanut butter and jelly sandwiches.

My transition out of solitude was so immediate, so rapid, that it was not a transition at all. In addition to Eric and his brother, I became good friends with a boy named David, who wore tinted eyeglasses, had a dog named Zorro, and whose father, the owner of Steeler season tickets, took me with him one Sunday to watch them beat the Rams. And there was Jay, with an extensive comic book collection and a very soft Afro he was enormously proud of and constantly grooming. "My hair!" he would cry out if I ever dared touch it, which I wanted to often. It was Jay's comic book collection that had compelled me to shoplift from that 7-Eleven where I was chased five blocks by the cashier—"Someone stop him!"—running, slipping, and hiding in the basement of Jay's apartment building. Then there was Erik, short, cherubic, dreaming of one day becoming a pilot, and who I had nicknamed Keebler—after those elves in the Keebler cookie commercials—so as to differentiate him from Eric. And finally there was John, gentle, soft-spoken, and the mastermind of amazingly inventive activities like treasure hunts and murder mysteries. On the weekends I would sometimes spend the night in his enormous red house, staying up past midnight, eating cookies and drinking soda, and then painfully rising at dawn to stumble along as he went door to door delivering the morning newspaper. It was during one of those sleepovers that he caught me scandalously masturbating beneath the covers.

"What are you doing?"

"Nothing."

"Yes, you are."

"No, I'm not."

No matter. To have seen me from above during this period would have been to see me weightless and unencumbered, frolicking through a Pittsburgh neighborhood, going from house to house, each open and welcoming, none concerned with my peculiar name or where I came from—even when I admitted that where I came from was Iran. Every morning, Eric would ring my doorbell and the two of us would walk to school together, sometimes meeting up with Keebler or Jay or John. Since they were all in other grades or other classes, I would generally not see them during the day, but in the afternoon we would meet up again and zigzag home, throwing footballs and snowballs, turning a fifteen-minute walk into an hour.

There was still no respite from the incessant, raging politics that continued to pursue my mother and me. The demonstrations, the *Militant* sales, the meetings, the emergency meetings, the conferences. These were the Reagan years, and the Reagan years were worse for the working class than the Carter years. The prospects had dwindled. The future had dimmed. There was the civil war in El Salvador, and the Contras in Nicaragua, and the eleven thousand striking air-traffic controllers who had been summarily fired. There was Reaganomics, the War on Drugs, and ten percent unemployment. This was the time when my mother left me home alone for the weekend so she could go to a disarmament demonstration at the United Nations. Within hours of her departure, I lost my keys somewhere in the playground and, unable to get back in my apartment, I spent the next two nights at Eric's house, happily eating peanut butter and jelly sandwiches and watching cable television. Now it was her turn to be petrified coming home to an empty apartment. "I was so worried when I didn't see you!" This was also the time I attended a special fund-raiser in support of something, or against something, and where, with my mother's consent, a comrade had slipped me a ten-dollar bill, whispering that I should announce I wanted to make a donation. "Why?" But neither my mother nor the comrade could answer why. Beneath a chorus of adult voices, I stood and shouted out, "Ten dollars!" All around me the comrades roared their approval.

Look, they shouted to one another, look, even the youth understand what we are up against.

One afternoon I dragged out all of the *Militant*s from the front closet and closed the door. The apartment was immediately transformed by that simple act. I had a sensation similar to the one I would get when our windows had been washed or our walls repainted and I would feel suddenly that I was living in an entirely different apartment.

On the living-room floor, I sat and proceeded to put every issue in chronological order. There were hundreds of *Militant*s, and many of them had grown faded and brittle and dusty. But there they all were: 1971, 1972, 1973 . . . The grape boycott, Watergate, the Vietnam War, coal strikes and teachers' strikes, the Equal Rights Amendment, desegregation busing. The *Militant*s were a chronicle of our lives, and as I put them in order it felt like I was reviewing a diary of sorts. I remember that demonstration, I would think. I remember that U.S. invasion.

I came across old articles and book reviews by my mother. "N.Y. mothers, children, occupy day-care office." "How day-care centers help children." "Nonsexist children's literature." And I found a photograph of my sister, taken when she was about sixteen, marching with a small group in front of the federal courthouse in New York City, holding a sign that read "Stop INS Harassment. No Deportations." In the photo my sister looks shabby, like a runaway, her long brown hair matted against her head from the rain, her clothes big and baggy, but there is still a smile on her face.

The job of organizing took hours, and the ink from the newsprint stained my fingers gray and then black. I had not planned well and I often lost track of which pile was which, or I would discover that I had two separate piles for the same year, or that I had mistakenly mixed various years together. I was determined, though, to finish what I had started, and I pressed on, ordering and reordering, the living-room air becoming scented with mildew and dust. As I progressed, the words lifted themselves off the pages and jumbled and danced and repeated.

"Struggle."

"Urge."

"Fight."

"Their fight is our fight."

"Hit."

"Strike."

"Crush."

"Killed 20,000."

"Killed 100,000."

"Killed six million."

"Nine-year-old black girl shot by Georgia racists."

"Help get the truth out!"

"We told the truth."

"Afraid to hear the truth."

"The truth about Afghanistan."

"We showed."

"We revealed."

"They lied."

"Lies, lies and more lies."

"Stop the lies!"

"End the lies and secrecy!"

"Open the doors!"

"Uncover."

"Distortions."

"Myths."

"Cover-up."

"The story they tried to keep from American people."

My eyes burned and glazed with these words.

When I was finally done, I waited eagerly for my mother to return home from work, and when she arrived at five-thirty she stood in the doorway, looking at the piles with delight.

"I can't believe it!" she said. "Look at what you've done!"

And then, together, she and I neatly stacked them up into bundles and tied them tightly with twine and carried them year by year back into the closet, until it was completely filled and the door once again was pinned wide open.

28

ALL GREAT REVOLUTIONARIES GO TO prison. It is a defining feature of their biography. It adds to their lore. It becomes them. Trotsky went to prison. So did Lenin, and Malcolm X, and Castro, and Che, and Debs, and Rosa Luxemburg. Jack Barnes has never been to prison, but there are always exceptions to the rules.

My father was arrested on November 21, 1982, on what must surely have seemed an ordinary enough day for him when it began. He had chosen that morning to pay a visit to the ministry in Tehran to respectfully inquire about obtaining a permit to restart printing his newspaper, *Determination.* The previous May he had been called in for questioning by the authorities and told he must cease publication at once. He had complied immediately with their demand, but now six months had passed—six months of political idleness— and perhaps my father thought he had detected something softening in the outlook of the clerics. So on that November morning he got out of bed full of hope and made his way through those hopeless Tehran streets, past the veiled women, the unemployed men, the uncollected garbage, the young boys heading off to war, and entered the doors of the ministry, hat in hand and without a necktie.

It was comrades in Iran who had told comrades in New York City who had told my sister who had told my mother

who had told me when I came home that evening from playing football.

"Mahmoud has been arrested," she said, sitting on her
bed in the living room, hugging her knees to her chin. Even
though it was dark, she had not bothered to turn the lamp
on and so her face was illuminated eerily, half in shadow,
half in light. I stood in the doorway, looking at her, my coat
on, my gloves on, stunned more by the mere mention of my
father's name than by the news of his arrest. How long had
it been since I had heard his name? It was my mother's face,
though, bloated with dread and slowly disappearing into the
darkness, that made unease spread through my body. It did
not matter how long it had been since I had heard his name.

Where was my father being held? What were the charges
against him? When would he be brought to trial? We did not
know. There was nothing we knew. Nor could we have done
anything if we had known. All we could do was wait.

And send a telegram.

"We're sending a telegram," my mother said the following
Monday in the middle of my breakfast.

I walked behind her into the living room. National Public
Radio was reporting on trivial and inconsequential matters,
and she reached up and turned it off. On the floor was the
phone, kept as it always was between a potted plant and the
bookcase, and my mother knelt down in front of it, her back
to me. The number was long and the process of dialing arduous, and she kept misdialing or kept being disconnected—
"Hello? Hello?"—and then she would have to start the
process over from the beginning, the long, slow uncoiling

of the rotary, many nines and zeros. "Is this where I send a telegram? Hello? I want to send a telegram to the president of Iran. That's right. Hello?" And then she waited as someone was being connected. "Yes. Hojatolislam Ali Khamenei," she said stiffly. "Hojatol—H-o-j . . ." The spelling of the president's name was like the dialing of the phone. Once completed, there was another long pause, longer than the first, as some mechanism on the other end was being put into place. Beside her on the floor was a prepared statement that someone from the party had composed. Instead of picking the paper up and holding it toward her face, she bent down to it, curling further into the ground, until she was in the shape of a ball.

"I am a supporter of the Iranian revolution," she read, "and an opponent of the U.S. government's threats against it." Her tone was firm and declarative, with a sharpness that made me wonder if the operator was someone who could be trusted. "I appeal to you for the release of Mahmoud Sayrafiezadeh . . . M-a-h . . ." And she commenced with the spelling of that odd first name and that even odder and more colossal last name, "S-a-y—S like Sam—a-y—yes, y like yellow—r . . ." Interminable spelling, exhausting everyone involved, especially the operator. When it had been spelled correctly down to the very last letter, she resumed.

"I appeal to you for the release of Mahmoud Sayrafiezadeh, who is currently imprisoned in Tehran. He is a member of the Workers Unity Party and a staunch anti-Shah and anti-imperialist fighter. He is innocent of any crime. I urge you to speed the release of Sayrafiezadeh—S-a-y . . .—which would strengthen the Iranian revolution in the eyes of the world."

Was that all? That was all. "Thank you very much," my mother said to the operator. When she hung up, she stayed kneeling on the floor, motionless, her head bowed. The piece of paper lay next to her, useless now, like a spent cartridge. I continued to stand behind her, over her, looking down at her back. It was the back of an elderly woman not yet fifty years old. I had the impulse to climb onto it like a monkey, like I might have when I was a little boy, but I knew that it would not withstand my weight.

It was the sound of the doorbell that roused us and returned us to Monday morning. It was time for school. I gathered my books while my mother hurriedly packed my lunch. Eric was waiting for me downstairs in the foyer, his face pressed against the window of the front door so that I could see the comic shape of his nose and lips smashed and widened.

"Look at me," he said through the window, "I'm a frog on the glass."

After sending the telegram, my mother and I did not mention my father's imprisonment again, treading politely around each other like roommates who share an awkward secret. At supper we talked about other things.

"How was school today?"

"Oh, pretty good, Ma."

"Did your math test turn out okay?"

"Oh, pretty good."

Days passed. One after the other. Just like the hostage crisis. Except this time no one knew but me. At Keebler's apartment playing Atari, or at John's house eating Twinkies, I carried the mystery silently. I even forgot about it from time to time. It was easy to do, as nothing in my life had changed. But when I returned home at the end of each day and unlocked the door and saw my mother standing in the kitchen making supper, I would suddenly remember everything. Today, I thought, today I will hear that he has been executed. And I would brace myself for the news, for my mother to turn to me with tears in her eyes and say . . . But, no, there was never any news. Each day was like the day before. How long would we have to wait like this? Slowly my anxiety began to change into something like expectation, and slowly the expectation changed into desire: I was desiring my father's execution—his final and permanent elimination from my life. It would be a spectacular end to the story, a fitting conclusion that would validate the power of his ideas, confirm his legacy, and add him to the pantheon. It would also give me a way to explain why he had disappeared from my life. He would be remembered as the man who would have been here if he could have been here. Death at the hands of one's captors was what every revolutionary aspired to; anything less meant they must have compromised somewhere along the way. When Che, weak and suffering from asthma, was finally captured in the jungles of Bolivia by the special forces he had brilliantly eluded for months, he remained defiant. "I know you are here to kill me," he told the soldier who had come to execute him. "Shoot, coward, you are only going to kill a man."

It was in bed at night, with my mother away at her meetings, that the haunted vision of my father suffering in prison would rise to the surface. Having no solid information to go on, my mind painted the canvas for itself. I pictured my father's prison, not as the infamous Evin Prison, where political prisoners in Iran were held and which Walter Cronkite would sometimes show us on the nightly news, but as the prison my mother had taken me to visit when I was nine years old. It was called Western Penitentiary and it was located on the north side of Pittsburgh, just a short drive across the Allegheny River. One winter afternoon my mother and I had traveled there to visit Stanton Story, a black man, about twenty-five years old, who had been sentenced to life in prison for killing a police officer. "Framed," my mother had told me. Twice he had gone to trial and twice he had been sentenced to death, but the Pennsylvania Supreme Court had voted to commute all death sentences and so his life had been spared.

Often when I was out walking somewhere with my mother, she would stop abruptly, remove a leaflet from her knapsack, and pound it into the telephone pole. *Free Stanton Story.* With a paragraph explaining the obvious injustice of his case, the racism of the police, of the media, of the American judicial system, and then a paragraph explaining how all of this was the result of capitalism. For as long as I could recall, Stanton Story had been a foremost cause for the Pittsburgh branch of the Socialist Workers Party—my mother and comrades had met with him on a number of occasions—and by the time of my visit, there was the real expectation that after four years of imprisonment he was on the verge of receiving a new trial and being released.

From the outside, the prison reminded me of my school, clean and modern. There was a brown garbage can at the front door that also looked familiar. Inside, we stood in a line of families waiting to be checked in. Once the guard had located our names on the visitors' list, my mother and I placed all of our possessions into a small locker, walked through a metal detector and then into a large room filled with men dressed in gray. The stories my mother told me had made me picture Stanton Story as a small, underfed teenage boy, but when he was led out to us I was surprised to see that he was tall, muscular, and handsome. He shook my hand with vigor. "I've heard a lot about you," he said. Along the wall we found three seats that faced out onto the crowded room. I sat next to my mother and my mother sat next to Stanton Story. The first thing she did was to bring him up to date on what the Socialist Workers Party was doing about his case: the meetings, the mailings, the protests. They were also planning to join with a black community group to have a car wash, where the money raised would be used to help offset Stanton Story's legal fees. This sounded promising. Then Stanton Story told her what the latest was from his lawyer regarding the police, the evidence, the witnesses.

Halfway through the visit, my mother gave me some change to buy a bag of potato chips for Stanton Story and whatever I wanted for myself. I wound my way through the men, women, and children to the other side of the room, where I came face to face with a row of vending machines. I dropped the coins and pulled the lever for Stanton Story's potato chips. Through the window I could see the bag being pushed to the edge and then falling over. Then I went straight to the ice cream machine, where pictures of all the various options were displayed, but I couldn't understand how to make my selection.

"We'll have to figure it out another time," my mother told me when I returned.

"That's okay," Stanton Story said, "I can show him."

So back I went, following behind him now. His clothes looked like pajamas. At the ice cream machine he said, "All you have to do is put your money in over here and then you push this button over here." Instead of putting the coins in myself, I handed them to him, but when I did he recoiled from me as if I had held a lit match to his skin. "I can't touch money!" he exclaimed. I could not conceive of such a thing. It sounded ludicrous, comic almost. But he had acted with genuine apprehension, genuine panic. Never before had I seen a grown man so panicked, and in turn I felt panicked. I reached up and quickly dropped the money in the slot and the machine registered its presence, and then Stanton Story asked me which kind of ice cream I wanted. "Chocolate," I said. And he showed me which button to push for chocolate.

When the visit was over, Stanton Story said a few words to my mother and then he shook my hand one more time. "I hope to see you again," he said. My mother and I watched as he was led through a door. The door had a window, so once it was closed we could see him standing there waiting for the guards to process some information. We waited while he waited. And soon I could hear the familiar sound of my mother beginning to cry, reaching into her pocket for a tissue, and muttering so only I could hear, "Goddamn fucking bastards. Goddamn fucking bastards. Goddamn fucking bastards."

Over the years the memory of that visit would pop into my mind at the most incongruent moments, and I would think of how Stanton Story was still sitting in prison, hoping any day for that new trial. While riding the bus to school, for instance, I would think, I am riding the bus to school and he is still in prison. Or while playing Ping-Pong with Daniel, or while walking through La Plaza de la Revolución, or, twenty years later, while sitting in Martha Stewart's office: I am making labels for potted plants and he is still in prison.

When the processing was all done, Stanton Story turned one last time and waved to us through the window, an optimistic wave, and I waved back. Then he was led through a second door and out of sight.

And so when I lay in bed at night, I imagined that it was in fact my father waving one last time before being led through that second door. What lay beyond that second door I could only guess. It was terrible, whatever it was. Not just hunger, fear, and sorrow for my father, but endless hunger, fear, and sorrow. An eternity of it. And nothing anyone, anywhere can do for you. Except send a telegram.

In December my mother and I celebrated my fourteenth birthday with a cake she had baked. The oven fogged the windows and the aroma filled the apartment. Fifteen candles burned. "One to grow on," she said. I ate two slices. Later I roamed through the apartment like a forest animal hunting for the gifts she had hidden. It was a game we had played since I was a little boy, and it always worked to prolong my anticipation to an exquisite, almost unbearable length.

"You're getting warmer," she teased as I danced anxiously around a corner of the room that concealed a surprise I could not for the life of me unearth. "You're getting so warm that you're standing by the sun."

"Here it is, under the bookcase!"

When I had finally found and unwrapped them all—a journal, an encyclopedia of baseball statistics, a calendar for 1983—I thanked her.

I was taller than her now and I had to bend down while she reached up to me, her arms around my neck, pulling me into her tightly.

"Happy birthday, Saïd."

That evening John came over to spend the night, and he also ate two slices of cake while my mother plied him with friendly questions. Alone in my bedroom, we came up with the idea to devise a short theatrical play, where one of us was an injured baseball player and the other his teammate trying to convince him to make a comeback. When we had perfected our lines, we pulled a chair in from the living room and invited my mother to watch the performance. She was a good audience member, attentive and appreciative, and John's voice was loud enough to be clear. At the conclusion, with the injured baseball player rising from his bed and declaring that he was going to give his career one more shot, my mother applauded heartily.

"Bravo!" she said. "Bravo!"

In January, it snowed and all the boys in the neighborhood gathered in the playground for a game of football. The concrete felt soft like a mattress and we tackled each other without fear of injury. The pristine whiteness was magnificent.

And when the snow melted a week later, Keebler, John, and I went on an exploration of the woods that ran along the railroad tracks. We spent the day thrashing our way furiously through the underbrush, stopping only to throw stones at the passing trains and to eat from a box of Froot Loops that John had the presence of mind to bring along.

And after that I woke one morning to the sound of the phone ringing. It rang only once. The conversation that followed was brief and muffled. "Saïd," my mother called. In the living room she was sitting on her unmade bed, her knees hugged to her chin, and without preamble she asked, "What would be the best thing that I could say to you right now?"

In a blink I rejoined, "That Mahmoud has been freed."

"Yes," she said, "he's been freed." And she smiled. And I smiled. It was light and uncluttered. The smile of a mother and son being reunited with their husband and father. Sixty-six days of separation. That was all. Not so terribly long when one thinks of how terribly long it could have been.

And thus ended my father's political career in Iran. There would be no more Workers Unity Party, no more *Determination,* no more run for office. Nor would there be any more Revolutionary Workers Party or Socialist Workers Party. The first Trotskyist party on Iranian soil, which had become three Trotskyist parties on Iranian soil, had finally become no Trotskyist parties. Khomeini had seen to that. A decisive victory. And for my father, a decisive defeat. He had been transformed into an ordinary Iranian citizen, a math professor at most, walking the streets of Tehran like everyone else, with nothing very special to do. Almost four years would elapse before my father was mentioned again, this time entering my life with a flourish as he delivered the stunning and unexpected news that he had decided to return to the United States, where he could once again take up the fight for a socialist revolution.

It was maybe a month or two after his release from prison that my mother showed me a little brown nut that had arrived for me in the mail.

"What is it?" I asked.

"A date pit," she said. And she told me that if I looked close enough I could see that in the center was my name carved in Persian.

I looked and could make out only indecipherable scratchings.

It was from my father, she explained, who had passed the time in his cell by whittling three date pits, one for each of his children.

"I'll keep it in this drawer for you," my mother said. "It'll be safe here." And she opened her dresser drawer and put the date pit inside and I never saw it again.

29

KAREN AND I ARE DATING. We're keeping it a secret from everyone at work, which makes it feel illicit and tantalizing. On the nights I go to her apartment in Queens, she'll leave the office just a few minutes before I do and then we'll rendezvous like spies on the subway platform. When we are sure the coast is clear, I will pick her up and swing her around.

Other nights I'll ride my bicycle down to the Village and meet up with her on Fourteenth Street, where we'll walk the few blocks to my apartment. "I wish I was a kitten so you could put me in your basket," she'll say. And I'll picture her small, fluffy, with a ribbon around her neck.

My studio apartment comes equipped with a dishwasher, a microwave, an air conditioner, a gym in the basement, and a roof deck from which I can see the Empire State Building. The rent is so exorbitant in my building that it is occupied almost exclusively by lawyers and bankers, who must think that I am also a lawyer or banker. Studio apartments, for instance, easily rent for sixteen hundred dollars a month. I, however, pay the unheard-of sum of four hundred twelve dollars, far less than for even the most dilapidated apartments in the Village. It is a deal that I landed by way of the New York City Department of Housing just two years after moving to the city, when I was earning almost no money. There were three thousand eligible applicants, I was told, but only sixteen apartments available. What a miracle it was when I opened my acceptance letter. Now I make a considerably higher salary but by law the rent cannot be raised, nor can I be asked to vacate. In twenty years it will revert to market price, at which point I have no idea what I will do next. For now I treat the apartment as if I own it outright and will live in it forever. I am its first occupant, and it is as spotless as the day I moved in.

Karen loves my apartment too and is appreciative of the little touches that I have made to it, like the lavender pillowcases, the cherrywood blinds, and, yes, the brushed-metal tissue holder. And at times she will offer insights of her own, such as "You should get rid of that lamp," referring to the black halogen floor lamp that I paid fifteen dollars for at Staples.

"I thought it was stylish and minimal," I said.

"It's not," she said. "It looks like a lamp in a dentist's office."

So one weekend we went to Filaments on West Thirteenth Street and selected a dark-brown lamp with a scalloped glass shade, for which I paid a hundred fifty dollars.

In the evenings we might work out in the gym where no other tenant is ever seen, making it feel as if it is an extension of my apartment. Or we might take a stroll down to Film Forum to see a movie. We hold hands and say nothing. The West Village, no matter what the weather or time of day, is always tranquil and romantic, the stately brownstones, the streets crisscrossing. Of all the streets in the West Village, I believe it is my street—Jane Street—that is the most beautiful of them all. And sometimes I will marvel at how far I have come from that street I once lived on that was also named after a woman: Ophelia Street.

Karen has begun making art again. Never mind the minor in marketing, never mind the job as project manager. The first thing you encounter upon entering her apartment is a giant easel wedged in by the front door. We bought it together and then spent two hours rearranging all the furniture to get it to fit. When I visit she'll show me the latest pictures she's drawn or the collages she's made. Once she collected various squares of toilet paper from bathrooms around New York City and then stitched them into a little booklet. "The patterns are quite pretty when you look at them up close," she told me. I had not known that toilet paper had patterns, but when I studied them up close I saw that she was right.

As for my acting career, I've given it up. The last audition I had was for a commercial for a video game that, had I been cast, would have shown me sitting in a tent in the desert, wearing a turban and playing Snowboarding Nintendo. "I'll get you next time, Snowboarding Nintendo!" I said in that same accent I use for every audition. In my mind I imagined Daniel and Tab, wherever they might be, laughing uproariously. Mercifully, I was not cast. And now I have moved on to playwriting, which is much better. In my spare time I sit home at my desk and try to conjure up interesting people who will say interesting things about the drama they find themselves embroiled in. I dream of stardom and a brownstone on Jane Street. Above my desk hangs the black-and-white photograph of my father standing behind the podium giving his speech on Che. Only the frame has changed, a custom black frame to replace the original brown one that had begun to splinter and sag after thirty years. When the guy at the frame shop opened it to remove the photograph, out fell the original label. "Happy Home," it read. "$1.37."

Karen is turning twenty-eight years old. When I meet her at the subway station I am holding a pink balloon. "I love pink balloons!" she claps. "How did you know?" Then she ties it around my handlebars. As we walk, it bobs back and forth.

At my apartment we order quesadillas and black bean soup from Benny's Burritos, because that's what she wants. While we wait for our food to be delivered, I surprise her with a bottle of champagne. "I can't believe it!" she says. I'm such a novice at opening champagne that the cork shoots past my face and half the bottle bubbles onto the floor. Karen thinks this is hilarious. I'm worried my floor will be stained forever. "Don't worry," she says, "it's parquet." I scrub and scrub.

When we're done with dinner, I go into the kitchen and take out an ice cream cake that reads "Happy Birthday, Candy." I call her Candy because the message on her office phone has always sounded to me like "Hello, you've reached Candy at Martha Stewart . . ." I stick two candles in the cake, the number 2 and the number 8. Then I light them and flick off the lamp. "Happy birthday," I sing. She whirls and shouts out in surprise. The 2 and 8 glow dramatically.

Her gifts are a big colorful book about the painter Chuck

Close and a fancy bar of soap. She flips through the book and smells the soap. "Mmmmm," she says. The soap is blue and has an engraving of a flower in it and comes in a wooden box.

Then I put the cake in the freezer, the dishes in the dishwasher, and the two of us ride the elevator up to the roof. We sit on a bench, her leg draped over mine, and we stare at the Empire State Building. Tonight it is illuminated solely in white, clean and austere.

"It looks nice tonight," I say.

"Let's sit and watch for the lights to go out."

"Okay."

"Thanks for the book."

"You're welcome."

"I like the soap."

"I knew you would."

"I'm not going to use it," she says. "I'm going to save it."

Karen is from Paramus, New Jersey. Born and raised Roman Catholic on Mayfair Road. Her parents have been together for thirty years. Chuck and Barb. They're schoolteachers, and they've worked hard all their lives. Their house is a cozy split-level with a garage, a garden, and wall-to-wall carpeting. Karen has told me stories about how, during the summer she turned eight, she watched her father cut down the apple tree, break up the concrete swimming pool with a sledge-hammer, and extend the house into the backyard. Friends, neighbors, and relatives came over to help. And the summer she turned twelve, he put on new aluminum siding while she stood next to the ladder and tied tools to a string so he could pull them up.

If I had walked past that house when I was a child I would have thought, *Look at them. The rich asses.*

About a month after we had started dating, Karen asked me if I considered myself a communist. "I guess so," I said. "What does that mean?" she wanted to know. So I began to explain to her how workers are exploited under capitalism and how wealth is concentrated in the hands of the few, but somehow we took a detour and got caught up in a discussion about whether or not under communism we'd be able to buy fancy soaps and beauty products and things like that. "Of course," I had told her, but I wasn't really sure. I wasn't sure if under communism the goal was for there to be overwhelming abundance or for everyone to have evolved to where they no longer desired material things. She didn't let the matter drop and asked me more questions that on the surface seemed rather elementary, like what's the difference between communism and socialism. Really I had no idea, but I gave a vague answer that socialism leads to communism, because that is what I remember my mother saying years earlier when I had asked her. But this did not satisfy Karen in the way it had satisfied me, and she went on with her inquiry. Continually flaring inside me was the impulse to respond either with generalizations, or various patched-together facts, or to just simply steer the conversation into familiar territory, where I could speak with some authority. To do this, however, felt immoral and unforgivable in the face of Karen's authenticity. Eventually I stopped trying to answer, and muttered to myself, "I guess I don't know what I'm talking about." And she had responded, more surprised than accusatory: "Yes, it sounds like you don't."

At midnight, and not one second later, the lights of the Empire State Building click off.

"Look! Look!" she says.

We stand and stretch our legs and I put my arms around her waist and pull her to me. Her head comes up to just below my chin.

30

ONE DAY, A FEW MONTHS before I turned sixteen years old, my mother suddenly did the unthinkable: She resigned from the Socialist Workers Party.

Just like that, it was all over. Simple and noiseless and done by way of letter, where she apologized and thanked them all the same. After almost twenty years of membership she had decided she had given all she had and could give no more.

There had been no indication she was considering such a thing. I did not even know such a thing *could* be considered. Only a week before I had seen her leave to campaign all day for Mel Mason, the party's presidential candidate. Behind the scenes, though, somewhere far out of earshot, a friend had casually posed the question: "Have you ever thought about what you would do with all your free time if you left the party, Martha?" That is how my mother had explained it to me. A friend's simple question had been enough to jog her into conscious action.

"I would be a writer," my mother had replied.

Now in the evenings and on weekends she wrote with determination, clacking away at the typewriter at all hours, writing and revising, until she felt satisfied and would drop a hopeful envelope in the mail to *Mademoiselle,* or *Redbook,* or to her brother—now teaching at Arizona State University—

asking for his critical feedback. And when the last issue of my mother's subscription to *The Militant* arrived in the mail, she did not bother to renew it. The years of accumulation had finally run their course. Not long after that, seeing no reason why we should have them in such close proximity, she asked me to move all the old bundled issues down to our storage unit. Which I gladly did, shutting the closet door and transforming the apartment. In the damp, dim, dusty basement I made room for them beside my comic book collection, my stamp collection, my teddy bears—all relics of the past.

And then our lives changed in another material way: We moved. To the apartment next door, which was smaller but had a sovereign bedroom that my mother would not need to cross in order to reach the bathroom. For the first time since I was eight years old, I would have some sense of privacy. The weekend before we moved, my mother and I walked over to the carpet store, where she splurged on a soft brown rug for my bedroom. Later I hammered a latch onto the door. There were no longer comrades we could ask to help us move, but that didn't matter; I was strong enough to do it myself. And so I did, dragging every single piece of furniture from apartment four to apartment five.

These were new beginnings for us: closet doors that closed, bedroom doors that locked, stories written late into the night. But two flights beneath it all, the *Militant*s remained. Sitting there in the darkness. Why exactly were we saving them? All those years never referenced. They could be bound and stacked and moved, but why could they not be thrown away? Because our allegiance and loyalty to the party, once so absolute, once so all encompassing, could not be undone by a mere resignation letter.

Which meant that when my teacher handed out blank ballots in my eleventh-grade scholars class and told us to choose—anonymously—the presidential candidate of our choice, there was only one choice for me. After we had each cast our votes, the ballots were collected by Mrs. Alexander, shuffled extravagantly, and then randomly redistributed back to us. One by one my classmates read the name of the candidate that had been ticked off on the anonymous ballot they held in their hands.

"Reagan."

"Mondale."

"Reagan."

Down one row of students, then another, then down my row, and I called off the name on the ballot—"Reagan"— and then on, one after the other, until there came an abrupt pause and the rhythm broke and Connie stared down at the piece of paper on her desk.

"I don't know," she said, almost inaudibly, "I think this might be a joke." And then she looked up, at a loss. "Someone has written in a name for president."

"Well, go on, Connie," Mrs. Alexander said, no doubt pleased that the paradigm of voting had been organically extended to include this possibility.

So Connie read the ballot loud enough for everyone to hear. "Mel Mason," she read, "Socialist Workers Party."

There was another pause, as if everyone in the room had inhaled at the same time and held their breath at the same time, and then, on cue, the entire class exhaled simultaneously and erupted with laughter. Long, loud, familiar laughter. Everyone in the room laughed, including Mrs. Alexander.

The envelopes that my mother mailed to *Mademoiselle* and *Redbook* came back with regrets. Determined, she sent others to other magazines, only to see those returned. Perhaps fiction is not your forte, her brother counseled, while he celebrated the publication of yet another novel to add to our bookcase. Into the night I would hear the dinging, the sharp fingers against the keys, the ding, the keys . . . but twenty years could not be redeemed in six months. Twenty years could not be redeemed in twenty years. My mother was the woman she was now, the woman who had become a secretary and then consoled herself as the years passed by basking in the sweet shade of belief.

"When will it come, Ma?"

"Soon."

"Will I be eleven?"

"No."

"Will I be eighteen?"

"Yes, Saïd. Yes. You'll be eighteen. When you're eighteen the revolution will come."

Eighteen was fast approaching.

31

THE LOCAL SUPERMARKET HIRED ME to bag groceries after school for $3.35 an hour. After a month it was raised to $3.45. It was an enormous supermarket, like an airport terminal, with endless aisles of fruits and vegetables, boxes and cans, stacked high onto the shelves. The manager was a hulking, white-haired man named Al Sandonata, who at first struck me as avuncular and then tyrannical. All the employees lived in fear of him. Early in my tenure he had berated me harshly about the forbidden process of "double bagging," and another time he shrewdly caught me punching in from my break three minutes late and put me to work cleaning behind the garbage compactor. My mother loved to hear these stories, delighted in them, as they confirmed everything she had ever told me about bosses.

In spite of Al, and in spite of the relentless tedium that comes with standing in one place for four hours a day and fitting objects into a brown paper bag, I actually enjoyed my job. I enjoyed the fact that I had good reason to be out of the apartment and away from my mother, and that I was required to wear a tie as if I were an accountant, and that I had to punch a clock as if I were a steelworker, and that food surrounded me like a mountain range—some of which I would steal. But mainly I enjoyed the cashiers. Especially Giuliana, pretty, dark, Italian, and five years older.

"Good afternoon, Saïd," she'd say when I arrived at her register, her accent making my name sound languorous and suggestive, making me happy to have a name like Saïd. "How was school today, Saïd?"

"Good afternoon, Giuliana," I'd say, trying not to stare at her lips. I'd kissed girls before, but I'd never kissed a woman and I wondered what it'd be like.

And for the next four hours we'd talk about my high school, and her college, and why Italy is better than the United States, and why the United States is better than Italy, an uninterrupted conversation that carried on as the customers arrived with their groceries, paid their bills, took their brown bags from me, and departed. In the background stood Al, perched behind his customer-service window like an owl, observing all.

If I was not assigned to Giuliana's register, I would do all I could to switch with the bagger who had been, and if I could not switch I would watch her as she rang up the orders, took the money, gave the change, every motion impossibly sexy. And when there was a brief interval between customers, five seconds of rest, she would turn and our eyes would meet.

One chilly evening about four months after I'd begun working at the supermarket, we both happened to be getting off at the same time and she offered me a ride home.

"Would you like a ride home, Saïd?"

The question made me hot. The heat made me shy.

"You have a car?" I said.

"No, silly, I have a bicycle."

It was beginning to rain as we left the store, and we ran

fast through the parking lot. I watched her brown hair swish from side to side. Inside her car, the drops pattered lightly on the roof.

"Tell me which way," she said.

"Go this way," I said. "I don't live far." I wished I lived far.

We glided over the dark and empty streets. My mother would be sleeping now, I thought. "Turn here," I said. "Go straight," I said. I watched her hands on the steering wheel, slender fingers, long red nails. When we arrived at my apartment building, instead of pulling in front, she looked around for a parking spot. Three blocks away she found one and parked the car but left it running. The rain tapped harder.

She turned a switch on the dashboard and the headlights went out. "I feel sad tonight," Giuliana said. Then she stared straight ahead through the windshield, her hands positioned on the steering wheel as if she were still driving.

"Did you hear," she said, "about those terrorists hijacking that Italian boat?"

I braced at the word terrorist.

"I think my dad knew somebody who knew somebody on that boat."

Yes, I had heard about it that morning, vaguely, indifferently, the news coming over the radio about Palestinians who had done something on a ship.

"That's sad," I said. Was I supposed to say something about the Palestinians' struggle for self-determination?

"They threw that Jewish man overboard. Did you hear that? That man in the wheelchair?"

"That's sad," I said again.

"The world is sad," she said.

We sat there saying nothing for a while. The rain let up a bit. Eventually she said, "I've thought about it, Saïd, and I've decided I'm too old for you."

"You are?" I said.

"Yes."

"I'll be graduating this year," I said.

That made her laugh.

"It's getting late," she said. "We should go."

She started the car but didn't drive off. I wondered if I was supposed to offer to walk the three blocks since now it wasn't raining so hard. Finally she leaned over, pulled me to her, and kissed me on the mouth.

That Friday night, Al caught me double bagging at Giuliana's register and threatened to fire me on the spot. "I'm thinking about firing you right this second," he said. He sounded like he meant it. The first thing I thought was that I'd never see Giuliana again. I looked at her, but she was pretending to be occupied with groceries coming down the conveyor belt. "Come with me," Al said. I followed behind obediently, feeling light-headed. His large frame cut a path through the crowd of shoppers. We stopped at the customer-service window, where he announced loudly and to no one in particular, "I'm going into the back room with Saïd. I'm thinking about firing him." A woman peeked her head out of the window and then withdrew it. The back room was packed tightly with the weekend's shipment. Pallets of boxes were stacked one on top of the other all the way to the ceiling. The night shift was lounging on empty milk crates, but when they saw Al they got up and made themselves busy. We stood between two towering columns of Pepsi.

"Why were you double bagging?" he asked again, this time as if he was just curious.

"I don't know, sir," I said. I didn't look at his face, I looked at his tie.

"Do you know how much paper bags cost?"

"No, sir," I said.

"Take a guess."

"Twenty-five cents?"

"They cost one cent each," he said, his voice rising. "How much would it cost if every bagger double bagged all day every day?"

He made it sound like it was a number I should be able to figure out. "I don't know," I said.

"Do you think it would add up to a lot?"

"Yes, sir."

"I'm thinking about firing you," he said.

"Yes, sir."

"What would your parents say if I fired you?"

My mother was sitting on her couch, writing in her journal by the light of the lamp when I got home. I told her what had happened. She nodded as if she already knew. "That's how bosses are," she said. "They threaten you with things like that to keep you in line." She shrugged. I went to my bedroom and latched the door. That night I slept poorly and woke before my alarm. It was six o'clock and I had to be back to work soon. When I opened my bedroom door to leave, I was startled to see my mother standing in the living room in her T-shirt and underwear.

"Your boss thinks you're an Arab," she said matter-of-factly.

"What's that, Ma?"

"I said, your boss thinks you're an Arab." Her face was pale and her eyes rimmed with red, as if she had been up all night reasoning it out. "He's Italian and he thinks you're an Arab and he's angry about what happened on that cruise ship."

"I was double bagging, Ma."

"I'm telling you!" she said. Her voice escalated and her hands punched the air, lifting her T-shirt slightly.

"Ma," I said. "Listen to me."

"No! Listen to *me*! I'm telling you!" And I could see her face transforming back into the old face of the party member, cracked with anguish and outrage over injustice, that face I thought was gone for good. Now here it was again, staring at me. I was frightened by that face, unsettled by it.

"Okay, Ma," I said, "I understand."

But she could not be placated. In that still Saturday morning, she screamed as loud as she could. "HE HATES YOU! HE THINKS YOU'RE AN ARAB! HE HATES YOU!"

"Okay, Ma, okay. You're right. Okay."

And after a while, convinced that I was in full agreement, she stopped yelling and regained her composure.

Finally she said, "You better get to work."

I made out with Giuliana one more time in her car before she confessed to having a crush on a twenty-two-year-old guy who worked in the produce section. "He'll be able to take me out to nightclubs," she told me. I wrote her a love letter, which flattered her but did not win her back. November arrived. The nights I was off from work I would eat supper with my mother. I no longer told stories about Al, but I would entertain her with anecdotes about customers and their shopping habits. "Tell me the one again about the guy who bought twenty-five loaves of bread," she would say. I would tell her and we would laugh and then we would fall into silence, just the sound of our forks scraping the plate. Sometimes I would look up and catch her staring out into space. "Ma," I would say. "Hey, Ma."

"What? . . . Oh . . . What?"

After supper I would go to my bedroom and latch the door and do my homework. Later I would hear the *ding ding* of the typewriter as she composed the stories that no magazine wanted.

Then one night when I returned home from work, at about eight o'clock or so, I found my mother already sound asleep in bed. She was lying on her stomach with the covers pulled up tightly around her neck and her face turned toward the wall.

She must be tired, I thought. And I went to my room.

The next morning, however, when I woke for school, she was still in bed, in the same position.

She must be staying home from work, I thought. She must be sick.

I ate my breakfast at the kitchen table just a few feet away from her, trying to be quick and quiet so she would not be disturbed. When I was done, I put my dishes in the sink, took a shower, dressed, and left for school, noticing she had not stirred once. And when I returned home that night, there she was in bed again. And the next morning too. I'm sure she'll be feeling better by tonight, I thought.

That afternoon, while my English teacher was trying to lead a class discussion, a principal's aide summoned me out into the hallway.

"There's a phone call for you," she said.

We walked quickly to the office, where I was led into a side room and left alone with a telephone. The call was from the fine arts dean's office, and the person on the other end was telling me they hadn't heard from my mother in two days. Was she okay? they wanted to know. I immediately pictured my mother in bed, on her stomach, her face to the wall, and it dawned on me that it was not the posture of someone sleeping.

"Yes," I said. "She's fine. I'll have her call you." I hung up. "I have to leave," I told the principal's aide. "I have to leave right now."

"I thought you would," she said with sympathy.

I left through the back door. It slammed shut behind me. Outside it was sunny, it was warm. Maybe the last warm day of fall. This is what it's like outside when I'm inside, I thought. I had the impulse to run, but running implied fear. Instead, I walked purposefully, one leg in front of the other. I saw myself arriving at the apartment building, climbing the stairs, opening the door, seeing my mother. Her body would be cold to the touch. The paramedics would tell me she had had a heart attack. "Two days ago," they would say. Years earlier an old woman had died in the apartment above us. The ambulance had come, lights and sirens, heavy footsteps on the stairs. Why hadn't this possibility occurred to me when I saw my mother in bed? Couldn't I tell the difference between someone sleeping and someone dying?

I could see my building now, just a block away, green and red trim. The windows of our previous apartment looked out onto the street, and I noticed the new tenant had put up flowered curtains. Maybe my mother would be at the kitchen table with her typewriter. "I just took a few days off to get this story finished," she'd say. "Try not to bother me." I put the key in the lock and the door swung open.

There she was, just like I had left her that morning: on her stomach, the covers around her neck, her face to the wall. It was the body of someone who had crawled in and then collapsed.

"Ma!" I shouted. "Hey, Ma!" She made no response. I put my hand on her back. Her body felt cold and stiff. "Ma!" I shrieked down at her. "Ma!"

And from very far away the words came: "What do you want?"

I took my hand from her. I stood up straight. "Are you okay, Ma?" I tried to sound calm. "Are you sick, Ma?"

No response.

"Wake up."

"Leave me alone."

"What's wrong, Ma?"

"You wouldn't understand."

"What wouldn't I understand?"

Again no response. I shook her back and forth. "What wouldn't I understand, Ma?"

At last she said, "You're the only good thing that's ever happened to me, Saïd. You're the only good thing." And she began to cry into the sheets.

Then the phone was ringing, clanging like an alarm.

I will tell the dean's office there's been a misunderstanding, that's all. Nothing to worry about. My mother will be at work tomorrow. First thing tomorrow, I promise.

"Hello," I said. I could hear the shaking in my voice.

"Hello, Saïd," said the person on the other end. "My name is Barbara. We've never met, but I've heard a lot about you. I'm your mother's therapist. How is she doing?"

"I don't know," I said. "I think she's sick, but I don't know."

"Can you put her on the phone for me?"

I pulled the phone over to her bed and put it to my mother's ear. "It's for you, Ma."

My mother took it with a spongy hand. "Yes," she said.

I went into the bathroom, but when I closed the door I

heard the phone ringing again. Was she going to answer it? No, she was back asleep, in the same position, as if nothing had happened.

"Hello," I said.

"Hello," said Barbara. Her voice urgent now. "I think your mother might have taken all of her medication. I'm sure she's going to be fine, but I need you to bring her in so we can take a look at her. Can you do that?"

"I can do that," I said.

She gave me the address. "I'll see you soon," she said.

I needed to call someone to drive us but I didn't know anyone to call, so I took out the phone book. It was heavy and sloppy in my hands. I'd never called a taxi before. I looked up the number. I dialed.

"We have to go, Ma," I said. "We have to go see your doctor."

I pulled the covers away. Her body looked swollen and wet.

"Can you get dressed, Ma?"

She groaned in protest but roused herself as if moving through clay. She sat on the edge of the bed in her T-shirt and underwear, blinking her eyes.

"We have to hurry, Ma." I took a pair of pants out of her dresser. "Can you put these on?"

She took them from me in slow motion and stood uneasily, teetering.

I bent down and lifted her legs, one at a time. Then I found a sweater and a pair of socks. When she was fully dressed, I went into my bedroom and took out thirty dollars from my drawer. It was all I had. When I returned to the living room, my mother was standing by her bed, holding a glass of water and a bottle of pills, drinking and swallowing. I snatched the bottle from her and put it in my pocket. She looked at me with disinterest. I had the urge to slap her face. My hand tingled with the sensation of it.

I brought her shoes to her, and she sat on the kitchen chair while I knelt down and put them on and tied them. Then we left the apartment. Her small, frail body leaned against me, yielding as I helped her down the stairs, two flights, past the basement door, past the letters in the mailbox, out into the sunshine. On the stoop we waited for the taxi, and after about a minute she folded over and lay on the concrete steps like a drunk woman. Two pretty girls walked by and looked at us.

The taxi arrived, and the driver came around and helped me get my mother inside.

"Thanks," I said.

"Don't worry about it."

The ride was surprisingly short. Ten minutes, maybe. When we got to the doctor's office the driver pulled alongside the curb. My mother had fallen asleep again.

"Wake up, Ma."

She woke and looked at me. The driver helped lift her from beneath her armpits.

"I can manage," she said sharply.

I handed him ten dollars and he took it.

Then we caught an elevator up some flights where Barbara stood waiting for us. "I'm sure it's been quite a day for you," she said to me. Her face matched her voice, composed, almost serene, framed by gray-blond hair.

We went into a room with a nurse dressed in white clothes. Barbara shut the door. My mother sat down in a chair and I sat beside her.

"How many pills did you take, Martha?"

"I don't care," my mother said.

I dug the bottle out of my pocket and handed it to Barbara. She opened it and looked at it for a moment. Then she closed it.

"Can you tell me what's going on, Martha?" she said.

The nurse started checking my mother's blood pressure.

"I don't want you to go," my mother said. Her voice cracked and she began to cry.

"Your mother has grown very attached to me," Barbara said. "I've decided to take a job in Virginia and this has upset her, as you can see."

A man with a tie entered. "I'm Dr. so-and-so," he said.

"He's a psychologist too, Martha," Barbara said. "I've asked him to come and have a look at you."

The man smiled at me.

"Are we going to have to commit you, Martha?" Barbara asked. "Is that what we're going to have to do?"

"I don't want you to go," my mother said again. Now the tears were coming harder, her mouth open, gasping for air. "I don't want you to leave."

"I need to know you're not going to try to kill yourself," Barbara said with the even tone. "Can you tell me that? Can you look at me and tell me that?"

"I don't want you to go," my mother said again. Her voice had the sound of a child's in it, and instantly I understood what was going on. This was the "friend" who had asked that question, "Have you ever thought about what you would do with all your free time if you left the party?" When had my mother ever spoken of a friend before? My mother had no friends. Had she ever had friends? Maybe there had been one or two in Brooklyn, but that was years ago, and after that there had been only comrades—and comrades weren't friends, they were something else, something deeper, something better. But this woman dressed in her slacks and jacket, looking like a businesswoman, was a *friend*. A friend who had helped my mother to leave the party. And now this friend was leaving too.

"I don't want to live!" my mother said suddenly. "I don't want to live anymore!"

"Don't say that, Ma," I said. "Don't ever say that!"

And now I was crying. The tears choking me in their haste to get out, running out of my face, dripping down my cheeks.

"I don't want to live," she said again.

"No, Ma!"

The nurse had stepped to the side now.

"What about your son?" the doctor asked. "Have you thought about what will happen to your son?"

"He'll be fine," my mother said, as if she had come to that conclusion a long time ago and was at peace with it.

"He doesn't look like he'll be fine," the doctor said.

And that is where we sat that evening in November, my mother and I in that doctor's office, both of us sobbing beneath a hard light, surrounded by all things white and stainless, as two doctors who were not dressed like doctors stared down at my mother with a mixture of impatience and pity, and a nurse waited nearby, and my mother, between gasps of breath, repeated again and again as if it were a mantra that would never find an end: "I don't want to live! I don't want to live! I don't want to live!"

32

THE SUNSHINE WAKES ME, THIN rays of light coming through the blinds. I was dreaming something, but I can't remember what it was. For a while I lie on my back and stare up at the ceiling, thinking about nothing. There are no sounds except the occasional howl of the winter wind. *Whooo. Whooo.* I pull the blanket over my shoulders so that only my face is visible. The blanket is thick and heavy and it presses down on my body as if it might be alive. I love this blanket and do what I can to use it in all seasons. On some spring or summer nights, even when there is no need, I will run the air-conditioning so that I have no choice but to sleep beneath it.

I roll over and look at Karen. Around her face and pillow, dark curls fall. There is no sign that she will wake anytime soon. Given the option, she would sleep all day if she could. I once witnessed her sleep twelve hours straight and still rise with regret. That's how she was as a baby, her mom and dad have told me. The photographs I have seen of her slumbering in her crib appear to bear that out. A chubby little girl on her belly with her mouth half open.

We've begun tentatively discussing the idea of moving in together. Wouldn't it be nice, we sometimes muse, to never have to pack a bag again to spend the night, to never have to say good-bye, to never have to be alone? Ever again. Yes, we say, it would be nice. But still the concept is fraught with what seems to me an intractable dilemma: I am loath to give up this small sanctuary I have carved out for myself on Jane Street. "I have an idea," I will offer at strategic moments. "Just move in with me here." And she will say, "No! It's just one room!" And then I will counter with a grand architectural vision that includes building a wall to cut the apartment in half. "No!" Just a few weeks ago, on a lark, we went with a realtor to look at a place on West Twelfth Street. It was dark, dirty, and three thousand dollars a month. There was also a horrible smell emanating, we feared, from somewhere inside the walls. The realtor blabbered on about the ample closet space while I moped, offered no constructive suggestions, and left feeling as if I might be coming down with something. "Don't worry," Karen consoled afterward, "we'll find something wonderful. You'll see." And I said, thinking that perhaps her defenses had been softened, "I have an idea . . ."

But I know she's right. Two people in one room is untenable. And one day, when we find a spacious apartment that is clean and beautiful, I will give up my sanctuary. And we'll move in together and we'll be happy together.

In the meantime, however, the thin rays of sunshine have grown stronger, yellower. And no matter how much I don't want to disturb her, it's time for us to get up and get going.

"Candy," I whisper. "Time to wake up, Candy."

She stirs and opens her eyes.

———

The subway is almost completely filled when we get on. I spy two vacant seats in the corner and I rudely hurry my way to them. Karen drapes her leg over mine as the doors close and the subway begins to hurtle onward at a ferocious clip. But the instant we reach the dark tunnel it slows, it crawls, and then it stops completely. A moment later the intercom clicks on and the conductor says, "Attention, ladies and gentlemen . . ." but what we should be attentive to is garbled and unintelligible. "What's he saying?" I say to Karen. Karen shrugs. By the looks of it, all the passengers have long ago resigned themselves to a slow and tedious trek uptown. We must resign ourselves too. The train chugs ahead to Twenty-third Street, then Twenty-eighth, then Thirty-third, doing in twenty minutes what should take five. I regret not having brought something to read. "We should have brought something to read," I say to Karen. There is a touch of reproach in my voice. Everyone else seems to have had the foresight. Around us, heads are buried in Bibles, novels, and newspapers, all in a variety of languages. Nearby is an elderly man dressed in a shabby suit and completely absorbed in a supermarket circular. Next to him is a mother halfway through a romance novel, her young son lying splayed across her lap, deep in sleep. Karen and I must pass the time by entertaining ourselves with the advertisements above our heads. We are particularly amused by the one where a doctor in a lab coat tells us of a fast and easy surgical procedure to remove all pimples, moles, and birthmarks. Ow, my leg has fallen asleep beneath Karen's. "Sorry!" she says. I drape it over hers. "Ow!" she says. "Your leg is too heavy!"

Finally we arrive at Eighty-sixth Street, where we gratefully make our exit. As we climb the stairs to the outside world, a crowd of people descends toward us, rushing headlong like tourists who realize their cruise ship is pulling away from shore. Karen and I are separated, jostled from side to side. Aboveground, the winter sunshine is brilliant and for a moment I lose sight of her. "Over here," she calls. We clasp hands and stand together on the corner, trying to orient ourselves as to which way is which. "I think it's this way," she says. "No," I say, "it's this way." Everything is suddenly familiar again: the coffee shop, the newsstand, the grocery store. This is the subway stop I would use when I lived up here on East Eighty-third Street. That is, I would use it when it was too snowy or rainy to ride my bicycle eighty-three blocks down to my part-time job on Houston Street. And then, four hours later, eighty-three blocks back up. I was twenty-four years old and had just arrived after wasting years in Pittsburgh thinking I could be an actor there. The most I could afford in Manhattan was a run-down, illegal sublet that had a claw-foot bathtub in the living room and a hole in the kitchen floor through which I could see the basement. On the first of every month I'd go to the post office and purchase a money order for four hundred two dollars and forge the name Linda O'Connor, who was the tenant of record. All my friends told me the apartment was a steal, that I was lucky to have it, and that I'd never find anything as good. At night I'd fall asleep petrified by the prospect that I was going to be woken by the landlord pounding on the door. I figured I'd have to live there until I hit it big with my acting career, but two years later I landed my miraculous deal with the New York City Department of Housing and packed up all my possessions and moved to Jane Street. And two years after that I got my job at Martha Stewart, making more money than I had ever made before. And not long after that a woman named Karen was hired.

The Guggenheim Museum is a popular destination on this Saturday afternoon. We stand in front of the entrance, waiting and looking, as people eagerly file past. The wind is beginning to blow sharply. "Are you cold?" I ask Karen. "Not really," she says. "Maybe a little." I put my arm around her and hug her to me. She shivers. A taxi pulls up to the curb and two people get out and two people get in. The people who get out ooh and aah at the odd white corkscrew museum in the middle of Manhattan. At the corner, a man about my age pretentiously puffs away on a pipe. "Who smokes a pipe these days?" Karen asks. "No one," I say. And not too far from him, standing beneath a lamppost, is a tiny old woman, barely noticeable, whose hair is gray, going white, and cut short like a boy's. She looks bewildered and slightly angry, as if she might be lost. A lost boy on the corner. The clothes she is wearing seem too big for her, even her shoes, and even her eyeglasses. On her back is a knapsack.

"Ma," I call out.

And she whips around as if a voice has yelled out "Fire." And then she sees me, recognizes me, and her expression of confusion changes into relief. A smile flashes across her face. "Saïd," she says tenderly, sweetly. I go to her. But the smile is already fading and her face furrows again with disapproval. "I've been waiting a long time," she says.

"I thought we said noon, Ma."

"I know," she says, "but I was afraid I'd be late and . . ." And now she is staring past me toward Karen. "Oh, Karen," she exclaims, "how have you been?" And she throws her arms around her and hugs her tightly, as if Karen were her daughter and I the wayward son-in-law she hoped she wouldn't marry.

"Norman Rockwell: Pictures for the American People." It was my mother's idea to come to New York City to see the exhibit with us. Fond memories of her father reading *The Saturday Evening Post,* she wrote to me in a postcard. The three of us ascend the spiral walkway, winding our way to the top. My mother moves with a sprightliness that belies her age. Nearing seventy, her mind is still sharp and her health is good. Karen has even remarked that she has a youthful voice. And her knapsack is filled with the possessions of someone who has a wide range of interests: novels and *The New Yorker,* pens and paper, a camera. It is her face, though, that tells the story. A drawn and haggard face, with sagging skin around the eyes, a downturned mouth, a constant frown like she is at all hours trying to work through a complicated problem. The face will light up at moments, will even laugh, but then it will return to that shape I know so well. And each time I see her she will seem as if she has grown smaller, more stooped around the shoulders. When I was a child she once made the mistake of telling me that it was normal for people to shrink as they grew older. I thought, of course, this meant that my mother would one day grow so small that she would disappear completely, and this frightened me and made me cry.

Inside the gallery, we are surrounded by large, colorful paintings so vivid they could be photographs. I had assumed they would all be the size of a magazine cover. "So did I," my mother says. We are all delighted. Here before us is an adorable little girl, nearly lifelike, wearing a red beret and holding her doll up to the family doctor, who examines it with his stethoscope. And here are three boys, partially undressed, running with terror past a wooden sign that reads *No swimming*. And here is a truck that can't get through because the dog won't move. We have entered a sentimental, idealized vision of America where all conflict is simple conflict. It has a calming effect. We walk quietly. The three of us side by side. Occasionally someone will offer a bit of observation. "Look," my mother says, "this girl's shoes are untied."

We spend a while marveling at a painting that shows a little boy, his mouth wide in disbelief, as he stands at the open drawer of his parents' dresser with Santa Claus's outfit in his hands. Titled simply *The Discovery*.

How funny, we say. How well it's been captured. How well it's been rendered. The boy is so alive, he looks like he might emerge from the canvas at any moment.

And then Karen tells us the story about the year she finally learned there was no Santa Claus. She was probably seven, she says, and it was just a hunch she had. But still she waited, smartly, until Christmas was over and all her gifts had been opened before she posed the question to her parents: "Is there really a Santa Claus?"

And her mother answered: "*We're* Santa Claus."

My mother thinks this is a sweet story. And so do I. And I throw my arms around Karen, imagining her as a little girl standing shyly in the kitchen doorway in her pajamas, asking a question that she doesn't really want to know the answer to.

The mood abruptly shifts in front of the painting of a little black girl. *The Problem We All Live With.* There is more to Norman Rockwell than just an idealized vision of America, the exhibit tells us, and he knows that not all conflict is simple conflict. The little black girl is being escorted by four federal marshals on what is presumably her first day at an all-white school, and scrawled on the wall behind her is the word *nigger.* My mother approaches the painting and peers at it closely. Her face has grown alert and angry, and it is etched with that familiar outrage over injustice.

"Do you know what this is about, Saïd?" she asks me. Her voice is cutting and it reverberates with accusation, as if I might have been the one to write *nigger.*

"Sure, Ma," I say, "I know what it's about."

After the exhibit, Karen and I take my mother to our favorite restaurant in the Village. It's a macrobiotic restaurant that serves dishes like kuzu stew and fried seitan cutlet. With the exception of the tofu soup, my mother's never heard of any of the things on the menu, but she's adventurous and lets us do the ordering for her. She's also never eaten with chopsticks and decides that tonight's the night she's going to learn. I give her a primer on how to hold them. "Like this, Ma," I say, shaping her hand, "put your thumb here and your index finger here . . ." But the food, once grasped, drops, and drops again, and soon I lose patience. Karen takes over. "Like this, Martha," she says, but even Karen's patience wanes, and eventually we give up and ask for a knife and fork.

When dinner is over and we're all stuffed with grains and vegetables, the bill arrives. My mother looks at it and then unzips her knapsack and removes an envelope filled with traveler's checks. She tears off four of them and sets them down. But the waitress has no idea what traveler's checks are. She must ask the manager. And the manager has no idea what traveler's checks are. He must make a phone call.

"Why don't I just pay with my credit card?" I say.

"No!" my mother says. "Let me pay."

When the manager arrives he says that, yes, they can accept traveler's checks.

And after that we go to Port Authority to see her off on her bus back to Pittsburgh. In the terminal the air is hot, the fluorescent lights are harsh, and an upturned cockroach lies in front of a vending machine. I can smell the fumes of exhaust. I hope to never ride on a bus again as long as I live. The chairs the three of us sit on are just a narrow strip of metal, barely wider than the average ass, that flip up automatically when you stand. They have been designed not for comfort but with the aim of keeping homeless people from sleeping on them. If you wish to lean back, you must lean against the wall behind you.

"What a fun day," my mother says.

"It was great," I say.

"It was great," Karen says.

And it is then that my mother asks, without prelude of any sort, "Saïd, can you tell me? How is Mahmoud?"

Her face blushes at the question, like a young woman's, like a young woman's at a dinner party in Minneapolis forty-five years ago. I should have been prepared for her to ask me this, since she asks it every time without fail. And every time, without fail, I find myself flustered and at a loss for how to respond. What should I say? He's doing just great, Ma. He's dating someone thirty years younger, Ma. Maybe if you'd been thirty years younger, huh, Ma? Or maybe if you'd been prettier, or smarter, or been able to keep up with his politics. Maybe then. Maybe then things would have worked out differently for you. For us.

But the fact of the matter is, I haven't seen my father for a long time. And most likely it will be a long time to come. And this embarrasses me and makes me resentful that she would ask. I did happen to talk with him on the phone a few months ago, and it was a pleasant talk, and he sounded so excited to hear about Karen and said he couldn't wait to meet her, but he couldn't right now, but soon, definitely soon.

"He's doing fine, Ma."

I was seventeen years old the summer my father returned from Iran. He told the Iranian authorities he wanted to attend a mathematics conference in California, but he had no intention of ever going back. The first thing he did when he arrived was to visit my brother in Detroit and my sister in Levittown, Pennsylvania, both of whom had resigned from the party by now and were working their way through college. He was supposed to come see my mother and me, but he never did. He found an apartment in New Jersey and a job teaching math in Brooklyn. And then he asked my mother for a divorce, since his new wife would soon be leaving Iran to join him. My mother consented, and thirty years of marriage finally came to an end.

We talked on the phone a few times. They were awkward, stilted conversations. I couldn't remember the last time I'd spoken to him, and I had no idea what to say. He seemed to take a keen interest in what I was going to do with myself now that I had graduated from high school, but I had no clue. Maybe work at the supermarket. Maybe get a job in a post office. I'd always heard that was a good job. What about college? he asked. I couldn't afford college. "I'd like to help," he said.

And the day I left to see him, my mother opened up that brown sugar jar and removed a fifty-dollar bill. "Don't let him pay for dinner," she said.

"Okay, Ma."

When the plane landed at Newark Airport, I was holding in my hand *Malcolm X Talks to Young People*. I wanted my father to see me with it. But something had gone wrong, a mix-up of sorts, and he was not at the gate as planned. Perhaps it was my fault and I had misunderstood. Not knowing what to do, I wandered aimlessly through the airport, looking for him.

"Saïd Harris," I heard a woman's voice say over the intercom. "Saïd Harris, please meet your party at such-and-such gate."

No one had ever called me Saïd Harris before. Even when I had desperately wanted to be Harris, I had remained Sayrafiezadeh. Now here Saïd Harris was being announced before thousands, as if he were the recipient of an award.

"Hello," my father said when he saw me.

"Hello," I said.

He was dressed in a white shirt and a blue tie and he looked just like the man in the photograph. We shook hands like friendly acquaintances. Then we got on a train and went to a restaurant in New Jersey to have our first dinner together.

It was an uncomfortable meal. I sat bolt upright in my chair the entire time and tried to act mature. The silences were long and deadly, and I blamed myself for them. Not knowing what to call my father, I was forced to wait until we made eye contact before I said something. *Hey, guess what!* He ordered red wine and I drank it and it went to my head. And then he ordered steaks. We talked about colleges and things I might study. Political science, I suggested. And we talked about plans to get together with my brother and sister.

He had no idea what I had gone through to get there for

that first dinner. The past lay beneath us, pristine and unexplored. He did not know that less than one year earlier I had dressed his wife—because she was still his wife—and taken her to the hospital. Nor, for that matter, did he know about the storm door I once hid behind, or the television cord I would hunt for, or the photograph of him that hung above my bed for years and years.

My mother never told my father what transpired that night when I was four years old and she left me alone in the apartment with the traveling comrade. I believe that is a crime tantamount to the crime itself. *The truth must not only be the truth, it must also be told.* Maybe she thought that such an unseemly development would have made our home less inviting were my father ever to consider returning. When she called party headquarters and told them what the comrade had done to me, they had responded, "Under capitalism, everyone has problems." Such an explanation, which I know my father would no doubt have endorsed, was apparently sufficient for my mother. And a few days later the party found another place for the comrade to stay. What had happened was never mentioned in our home again. It was up to each of us to bear our private miseries alone, until that glorious day in the future when it would all be resolved once and for all, and a perfect world would emerge.

My father wouldn't let me pay for dinner that first night. He wouldn't hear of it. The fifty-dollar bill sat heavily in my pocket. And while we waited for the waitress to arrive with my father's change, he removed a small photograph from his wallet. "Look," he said. It was a small black-and-white photograph of me as a baby in the old Brooklyn apartment. I am on my belly, raising myself up by my arms, and I am smiling at the camera.

"I've carried this with me the whole time," my father said.

My mother's bus has arrived.

"Good-bye," she says to Karen, giving her a hug and a kiss.

And then she turns to me. "Good-bye, Saïd."

"Good-bye, Ma," I say.

And suddenly she throws her arms around me, clutching me around the shoulders, dragging me down into her.

"Good-bye, Saïd," she whispers, but she is crying now and the words can barely be formed.

Before I can say anything more, she picks up her knapsack and boards the bus. A line of people board behind her. Through the tinted window I try to find her. I think I can see her waving. I wave back. And soon the bus is filled, and the driver closes the door with a whoosh, and it pulls away toward Pittsburgh. We watch it pull away. The smell of diesel lingers.

And after that, we walk down to the subway station, Karen and I, where we get on the train, she drapes her leg over mine, and we rumble beneath the city back toward home.